Energy 101

The Key To Understanding

Holistic Health

ISBN 1-931391-85-8

Published 2001

Published by Jan Meryl, P. O. Box 683, Sarasota, Florida 34229, USA.

Manufactured in the United States of America

Booklocker.com, Inc.
2001

Energy 101

The Key To Understanding

Holistic Health

Jan Meryl

Energy 101

The Key To Understanding

Holistic Health

About the Author

Jan Meryl is a holistic medical intuitive, a psychic consultant, and a hypnotist. Her intuitive readings present channeled information from angels and spirit guides, spirit communication, and holistic, energy field health scans. Since beginning her career as an intuitive, fifteen years ago, she has assisted thousands of people in discovering and using the full potential of their own creative powers for personal growth and self-healing. Jan has an M.F.A. degree from Florida State University and has exhibited her paintings throughout the state of Florida. She currently resides in Sarasota, Florida.

Dedicated with love to Spencer

Table of Contents

Preface

Information is power. I wrote this book to share the higher teachings of the spirit guides with anyone who is interested in obtaining this type of information. Every day I learn something new. Therefore, new articles, scheduling information for workshops and readings, and contact information are available on my web site. The URL is http://members.aol.com/Readings4u.

Introduction

At the age of twenty-two I came face to face with death. I was on a two-lane road called Alligator Alley. The road connected the east coast of Florida to the west coast, and it was surrounded by swampland. It would take almost three hours to complete the drive. The road contained only a couple of exits that led to an Indian reservation located somewhere in the middle. Consequently, once my journey began, there was no way to turn back.

There was a light drizzle when I drove my red Ford Falcon onto the Alley to begin my journey home. However, ten minutes into my drive, the afternoon skies exploded. Looking out of my windshield all I could see was a wall of water. My windshield wipers were old and useless, and I could not see beyond the inside of my car. Although my life had hardly begun, I made my peace with God and decided that since I had no choice, I was ready to die. I drove on and waited for my final moment.

It was by the grace of God that my car did not veer off the road into the swamp. I remember thinking that there wasn't any point in steering the car because I could not see the road, when suddenly, out of nowhere, a flashing yellow light appeared directly in front of my windshield. I followed the yellow light through the deluge of water for about twenty minutes. When the rain began to decrease enough for me to see out of the car, the yellow light mysteriously disappeared. Where could it have gone? If it was coming from a vehicle, there was nowhere for it to have exited the roadway. When the angels come to the rescue, they leave behind a distinctly mysterious feeling to an event.

By all logical accounts, that was my day to die, but I didn't. Instead, I went on to live what appeared to be a very normal life, with a sparse sprinkling of surreal experiences and spiritual communications until the day arrived that turned my "normal" life upside down. I reserved my account of that day for the first page of this book. Needless to say, after my premature, unexpected confrontation with death, something inside of me knew that my life would reveal that there was a reason why I had experienced that miraculous rescue.

In hindsight, I believe that the entire drama was created in the spiritual realm and implemented on the earth plane to send a message to me that my life had a purpose. From that day forward, I knew that I had an important destiny, although I did not have a clue as to any of the details. I merely knew that I would not die, and could not die, until my contract with God was completed.

The impact of that day was very strong, but after awhile the memories were stored away in my permanent memory files. Only now am I beginning to reflect upon that apparent rescue and connect it to the results of my intuitive work. Now that I have done thousands of personal intuitive readings, I look back to that terrifying and enlightening day and say, "What if I had not lived to do all of these readings?" I can speculate that there are some clients that have come out of a reading thinking and feeling no different than when it began;however, there are also so many people that freely express the positive effects that the readings have on their lives. It is not uncommon for me to hear someone say, "Your readings have changed my whole life for the better. I don't know where I would be had I not found you." I feel blessed to be given the credit for being the voice of the angels and spirit guides.

Based on my readings and personal meditations, I have created a comprehensive description of who we are and how we function, which clarifies how and why we create personal reality on the earth plane. This, I believe, is a large part of my soul agreement. It is my destiny to learn and share this higher knowledge, presented to you in the form of this book called **Energy 101: The Key To Understanding Holistic Health**.

To those of you that have experienced my readings, here is the book that I promised you. I hope that it fills in the missing pieces and gives you an understanding of the underlying dynamics of energy. It is impossible to fully convey all of this information in the short time that we spend together in a reading. For those who read the book that have not experienced my readings, I hope that you can apply the knowledge gained from this book to your life and use it to your advantage. Perhaps it will light the way for you to discover your destiny too.

Part I

The Big Picture

Chapter 1

My Story

I know not of the road I take,
I know not where it leads,
But if I stumble and I fall,
God will know my needs.

I was a reliable, helpful, loyal daughter for thirty-seven years, a loyal, hardworking wife for twelve years, and a loving, conscientious mother for six years. One day, I volunteered my time to help hang paintings for a local fair. I had a terrific time working with a fellow artist into the evening hours. Before long, I noticed that I was purposely avoiding calling home because I feared that I would be asked to leave the fairgrounds. I was having carefree fun for the first time in many years. I returned home at 10:00 P.M. to an overly excited family. My husband and parents were all talking to me at the same time. They presented me with exaggerated claims about how difficult and nearly catastrophic the day had been because I was unavailable. This assignment of blame sounded preposterous to me.

For one isolated day, I found freedom and joy outside of the family group. Serving as an enabler to all of the members of my family, I had not, until that day, put any energy into enabling my own self-expression and personal growth. Previously, I had allowed the endless needs of my parents, husband, and young child to harness all of my time and attention. In my mind, I was doing everything that a good wife, daughter, and mother should do. Continuously busy with the demands of my family, there seemed not to be any time left over for me. Taking responsibility for my own happiness was a non-existent concept. The joy, freedom, and fulfillment that I felt the day that I broke my pattern were diametrically opposed to the reaction that I received from them when I surprised them with my unpredictable lack of availability.

I had broken tribal law. By not calling home throughout the day, I had not acted the way that my family had taught me to act. I had selfishly made my self-interest a priority. My change in behavior made a silent statement that I was beginning to take the responsibility for my happiness out of their control and place it within my own. Their absurd behavior was a clear sign of disapproval and an attempt to sabotage any future efforts to repeat the choice to recall my personal power.

I was on the brink of a huge revelation. Although they loved me, my family was not serving to enable and empower me at all. The fact was that they did not know how. They were living and perpetuating life as they knew it. Co-dependence was comfortable for them. They were experts at knowing how to need and be needed. The tug of war over my energy was only beginning. I was learning that becoming responsible for one's own energy is a personal journey and also a very scary thought. I bit the bullet.

I felt them clutching, like a cat whose claws grip into your skin. I retreated down the street and looked up seeking to find God in the beautiful night sky. "There is definitely something wrong here," I said to God. Apparently I was right. God must have taken it as a request to fix the problem because from that moment on, everything in my life changed.

I had many spiritual psychic experiences prior to that night, including astral travel, a pattern of having visions of pieces of events of the following day, two eerie near death experiences that looked and felt like miracles, and a full color, inner vision of the face of my Native American spirit guide in a full headdress. Still, I never dared to imagine the series of events that were to follow.

I remember feeling a snap in my back on that starry night. With my eyes closed, I watched a door rise up on my inner visual screen and in my gut I felt a deep sense of knowing that wherever I was headed, I could not go back.

A few days later, I began hearing an inner voice that was willing to dialogue with me, guide me, encourage, and support me in my new found moments of extreme devastation and confusion. The days and weeks that followed revealed that my life, as I knew it, was in rapid disintegration and fast-forward. I pleaded for answers. "Why? Why is my life falling apart?" I was simply told, "You will know," and then given the opening poem to fall back on in my moments of severe doubt. Although this short poem may seem like a mere morsel to you, it was a lighthouse in a storm to me.

After fifteen years, the pieces of the puzzle are fitting together into a complete picture that I now understand. My life, up to that unpredictable, climactic moment, had been based on hit and miss behavior. I, like most of us, did not have a clue about how to use energy to create health and happiness. My spirit guide informed me years later that had I stayed the course, I was headed for a good solid case of cancer. I will never be able to verify the truth of that bit of information because instead of clinging to my dysfunctional life, I took the hand of God, by that I mean that I looked inward for my power, and chose instead to listen to the voices of my spirit guides that advised me to follow my heart and foster my abilities.

I began to paint with the determination that I would not stop learning how to do it until I felt that I had reached my full artistic potential. This was my childhood dream, the one that I continually put off to satisfy my fears and everyone else's endless needs. I enrolled in graduate school for a Master of Fine Arts degree and began using my newly enhanced psychic abilities to channel from the voices of angels and spirit guides for the mutual benefit of myself and others that shared my belief in these entities.

Fifteen years later, I can say that I have done thousands of readings. I feel very fortunate and grateful to have access to the loving, intelligent energy that emanates through the dimensions, transmitted from wise master souls through the doorway to human consciousness. As if peering through the back of a one-way mirror, they communicate to me what they know to be true. In the following pages you will find an organized exposé of all that I have seen, heard, and understood from these spirit guides in my many thousands of personal channeled readings.

This book contains the invisible, unprovable truth. I do not ask you to believe this information. I merely present it to you as a philosophy for your own choosing.

BEAR WITH ME. WHAT I HAVE TO SAY NOW MAY GO AGAINST EVERYTHING THAT YOU HAVE EVER BEEN TAUGHT.

The goal of this book is to shed light on who we really are, and what we really need, as opposed to whom we think we are, what we think we need. As a species, it is time that we stop feeling like victims of outer circumstances and learn to identify our choices of thoughts and beliefs that manifest into unacceptable situations. We must learn to create alternative solutions to our own problems, rather than depend solely upon constant prayer requests to be saved.

By learning to ask the proper questions to ourselves, we can begin to access information that we carry within our own energy fields about how we participate in creating our own health, happiness, illness, and misery. By learning about the architectural structure of our energy fields, and the forces that underlie the dynamic movement of energy through our energy fields, we can begin to understand how and why we function as we do. With this knowledge we can make the changes necessary to increase the quality of our lives by turning the process of living life from an unconscious, diseased, lonely, needy, fear based, immature journey, into a mature, responsible, conscious, expansive, fulfilling one. By learning the energetic laws of the universe and how they mold our energy into manifested reality, we can begin to make some sense out of the apparent chaos of our lives. When we learn how to recognize the causal order, we can evolve more rapidly from feeling like powerless victims to understanding our part as conscious powerful creators. When we begin to take more responsibility in the production of our own energetic manifestations, we will access a higher level of joy and satisfaction heretofore unavailable to us as human beings.

Chapter 2

Who Are You?

You are me and I am you. We are made up of a singular, indivisible, intelligent energetic force. We are one spirit taking the form and appearance of separate individual entities. All matter creates the illusion of being separate form, but within each form, every subatomic particle and wave is alive with intelligent, interconnected, spirit energy. Throughout this book I have used the terms Spirit Energy, Spirit-Self, God-Self, Oneness, Whole-Self and All Is One interchangeably to refer to the unified, energetic, creative force.

In his book on the science of quantum mechanics, Gary Zukav talks about the ubiquitous wholeness when he states

> "all that exists by itself is an unbroken wholeness, that presents itself to us as webs of relations....The physical world, according to quantum mechanics, is ...not a structure built out of independently existing unanalyzable elements, but rather a web of relationships between elements whose meanings arise wholly from their relationships to the whole."

When describing the qualities of the new science Zukav says,

> "the philosophical implication of quantum mechanics is that all of the things in our universe (including us) that appear to exist independently are actually parts of one all-encompassing organic pattern. We are never really separate from it or from each other."
>
> Gary Zukav, *The Dancing Wu Li Masters*

Because everything we see with our eyes appears to be separate from us, it stands to reason that we would seek to relate to a creator God as a separate identity too. But, things are not what they appear to be. In truth, all the while that we have been blaming our life circumstances on an invisible outside force that we call God, the universe, or chance, we have actually been manifesting our own personal external realities through the unconscious use, or misuse, of our own internal energy. Perhaps it is difficult to believe that you are constantly using the power of the God-Self to create your own unhappy circumstances because you wonder how and why you would create, illness, difficulty, and loss. My answer to you is that your soul, along with all the other souls on this planet, is choosing to experience what it means to be human.

Being Human

What does it mean to be human? Being human means to experience feeling like a separate individual. I shall use the term ego-self, to refer to the self that perceives itself as separate from the whole. In order to feel separate, one must turn off the spiritual light that shines on the indivisible wholeness of the Spirit-Self. We do this by forgetting the truth.

Once the lights are turned off, turning them back on and functioning from a state of wholeness, rather than from the ego-self, is very difficult to do. The catch is that everything and everyone that appears to be outside of you will invite you back into your ego-self perspective, including organized religion. The temptation to believe the separateness that we see with our eyes will always be in front of us. This apparent separateness is the root of all of our doubts, fears, and insecurities that motivate our uncontrollable, undesirable behavior and circumstances.

Who Turned Off the Lights?

There is a myth that provides an answer to this question. The myth tells us that as a whole, unlimited, and complete being, God got bored. God thought, "I am all there is. I contain all possibility and all potential. I am complete fulfillment. This is what I am. This is what I always am. But, I am bored." What do we do when we get bored? We imagine something different. God imagined something different. God imagined, "What if I were not what I am?" In an instant it imagined itself experiencing what it was not. So, in a playful mode, the God-Energy, which is us, created the thought of separation from its unity, which is a negation of what it is. It left the truth of itself behind and went on a little imaginary, fun filled vacation. By denying its unity, it turned itself inside out and entered a very scary fun house of unlimited possibilities. God imagined time and space in which to experience what it is NOT. The Bible states,

> "And God said of every tree of the garden thou mayest freely eat; but of the tree of good and evil thou shalt NOT eat of it; or in the day that thou eatest thereof thou shalt surely die."

What is being said is: Do NOT split the wholeness into duality, for if you do there will be death to the unity (there will be separation) and that will cause conflict and imbalance. Conflict and imbalance inherently create dynamic movement. When we choose to deny our unity, for the purpose of having human experiences, the constant unchanging stillness and peace of knowing that we are the "All That Is" is gone. And so it is.

O

ALL THAT IS = A SINGLE WHOLE

Think of duality as a line with two sides. The ends represent two opposite concepts. Yin and yang, heads and tails, right and left, inside and outside, good and bad, are all examples of duality. Now, think of the line as a rope, where the two ends can come together to form a circle. In a duality, the two opposites join to form a single whole. When we experience both sides of a dualistic concept, we gain a whole, complete understanding of it.

LIGHT ______________ **DARK**

YOU ______________ **ME**

INSIDE ______________ **OUTSIDE**

DUALITY

EXPERIENCING BOTH SIDES OF A CONCEPT CREATES A FULL UNDERSTANDING OF THE WHOLE CONCEPT

The Human Paradox

Allow me to summarize the human paradox. While you and I appear to be two people, you and I are actually one singular, indivisible, spirit energy. Albert Einstein showed us that $E=MC^2$. Energy becomes matter and matter changes into and out of multiple forms, but it always continues to be energy.

Our earth plane is set up to support the perspective of the separate ego-self and negate the truth that we are one indivisible, whole, Spirit-Self. This denial of the larger truth is the source of our identity crisis and our constant inner conflict. Just as the grain of sand in the oyster produces a pearl, the discomfort of this denial of the true, unified self instinctively leads us on a path to search for the light of truth. When we are able to recapture it, we rediscover who we really are. This process constitutes the spiritual journey.

For example, if I were to turn on a flashlight in a well-lit room, the beam of light from the flashlight would not be visible. But, if I were to turn a flashlight on in a totally dark room, you would easily see the beam. When you see and know yourself as a separate, individual, ego personality, you agree to negate all that you truly are. Turning off the light is the equivalent of saying, "I am NOT the Creator, we are NOT one, and I do NOT have that kind of power." The earth plane becomes a place where you can rediscover your own inner light, which is the creative power that comes from your internal connection to the Spirit-Energy wholeness. Learning to see beyond the illusion of separation is the circular, spiritual journey that takes us home.

Life Is A Spirit Game

We are continuously deciding whether to dream on with the illusion of separation, which is to leave home and continue the vacation, or whether to complete the trip by returning home to the knowledge of our creative power and unity. Each time I choose to affirm my true power and unity, I dismantle the foundation of the fun house which I, or rather, You -We, built for the purpose of experiencing the "NOTs" of being human, Therefore, it is crucial for the ego-self to keep reaffirming a negative perspective in order for the psyche to believe in separation and stay in the human, dualistic, experiential game.

As I have said, the cornerstone of this illusionary earth plane is dualism. We are here to invest belief in and experience what we think we are NOT (whole and complete). On this earth plane we must experience the negative without which we cannot know the positive. The meaning of each side of duality is derived from the relationship between them. We are here to understand poverty in relation to wealth, illness in relation to health, short in relation to tall, and happy in relation to sad.

"NOTs" in the Energy Field

Beyond the initial, "NOT" whole and complete, what exactly are those personal dualistic "NOTs" that invite our attention in the physical world of separation? They are those things which, as human beings living in a body, give us knots in our stomach. As individuals, we can feel NOT good enough, NOT valuable, NOT rich enough, NOT in control, NOT loved, NOT appreciated, NOT powerful, and NOT healthy. In the physical world, we can perceive both an interior and exterior world. We can see, feel, and touch things outside of ourselves. As separate ego personalities, we can experience feelings of need and lack. We can also have the experience of feeling anticipation of loss, which is fear. We can ride the wave of fear and use it as a motivational force, ever convinced that there is actually something to fear outside of our own perception of being separate, small, and powerless. We can choose to give these feelings the power to rule our lives.

With the arrival of the perceived separate other, we create roles and relationships such as: mother, artist, singer, hero, teacher, king, friend and enemy. We can attach judgments such as: guilt, sin, good, bad, right and wrong to people and their actions. We can create concepts of good and evil and build religions where we find someone or something to worship. Then we can assign good qualities to the idol and bad qualities to ourselves so that we have a reason to affirm more separation. We can compare, and we can judge each other, do to another or take from another. Conversely, we can feel blame by accusing another of doing something to us or taking something from us. We can create reasons to feel powerless and call ourselves victims. Oh, what fun we can have with this concept.

With our bodies, we can play games and create challenges. We can compete and experience concepts of winning and losing. We can push limits and break records, over perform and under perform, experience success and failure. We can seek to achieve more. We can feel better than and less than. We can yearn for validation from another, mistakenly thinking that it is the answer to the feeling of NOT being good enough. We can fly on the wings of love and crash land on its demise, while we blindly cling to the false belief that there is actually somebody else out there to love. On the illusionary holodeck, as separate ego personalities, we can both observe and create the meaning of being human by coping and juggling with the "NOTs." We can dance the dance of life by allowing ourselves to deeply feel all the emotional highs and lows. This is how we experience the hands of time. We flow with the constantly changing appearance of what is and what is NOT.

We search, theorize, and debate with the hope of unfolding that profound inner secret held deep within our gut that we can feel but just cannot reach. All the while that we are looking for and creating some universal or personal meaning, we know something is missing. There must be more. If only we could access it. Whatever it is. We canNOT. We have those illusive feelings of potential inner peace and self-love that come and go, as we wonder, "Why can't we hold onto them?" We feel like outsiders who have lost the key to the door that shuts us out of the knowledge of our true identity and purpose.

The illusory world of separation takes the energy of "All That Is" and makes it appear to have gone through a meat grinder. No wonder we feel so lost. How can we ever put Humpty Dumpty back together again? Can discovering the indivisible, whole, creator, Spirit-Self be the profound illusive purpose that gnaws at our belly? Can this be truth calling us home?

The "I AM" List

of the whole creative Spirit-Self

A Higher Perspective = Remembering Who You Are

This is a list of what we know, feel, and believe from the perspective of a unified, singular energy. This is the knowledge that we carry when we identify with the creator God-Self. Each of these thoughts carries a positive electrical charge.

- God-Energy is unlimited, whole, and complete. Therefore, I am whole and complete.
- I know that "I am that I am." My tribe is the universe.
- The thought, feeling or belief that something is NOT there is false.
- I know that the whole of what I am exists in peace and perfection.
- I know that God-Energy expresses through the personality in the world of form.
- I know that I have the power and ability to access the voice of God-Energy internally when I can quiet my individual ego-voice.
- I know that there is an underlying order and perfection.
- Everything that appears separate is interconnected and communicates in simultaneous time.
- I know that I am on the physical plane to experience duality and rise above it.

- I know that having a thought or belief is the simultaneous energetic way to create an experience. I accept and understand my innate power to create.

The "I Am NOT" List

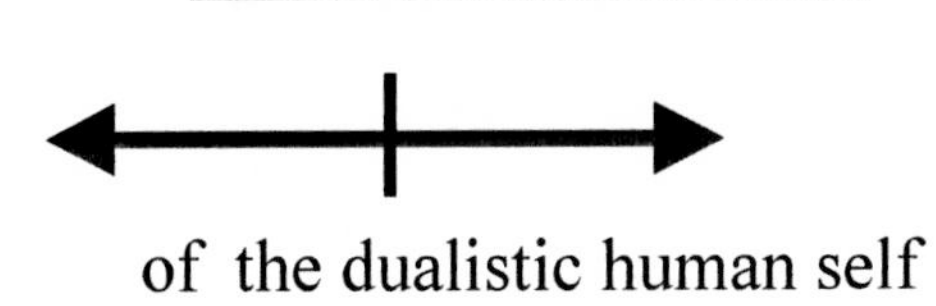

of the dualistic human self

The Veil of Denial of Internal Creative Power

This is a list of the energy that is carried when one identifies with the separate ego-self that perceives itself to be lacking. This is the list of issues that emerge within the human condition. Negative energy is created with every denial of the truth of the existence of internal creative power and wholeness. Each NOT contains a negative electrical charge.

FEELING **PERCEPTION**

I feel and/ or know that something
is missing in my life.................................. NOT whole

I feel powerless to change my
external circumstances.......................... NOT powerful

I am focused on getting and
achieving what I do not have.........................NOT having = lack

I am focused on satisfying
the needs that I perceive I have.......................NOT having =lack

I fear the loss
of what I have ....NOT safe & secure

I fear being
controlled by another.................................NOT in control

FEELING	PERCEPTION
I fear not having money and security	NOT safe & secure
I fear being alone, unloved, and unappreciated	NOT loved, valued and supported
I don't have any reason to feel valuable.	NOT worthy
I must prove my worth to others	NOT owning worth, esteem
I am not good enough	NOT good enough
I feel and create judgment, guilt, and blame	NOT good enough
I fear being judged by others	NOT self approving

When we decide to go on vacation from the unified truth of who we are, we pack a suitcase full of the preceding human issues.

How We Block Out the Light

The unified energy's purpose is to hide our true singular identity and to create a mechanism with which to experience the "NOTs" of whom we are. Spirit-Energy is working in many ways to accomplish this goal of deception. First and foremost, a body is created that appears to our senses to be a completely separate and autonomous piece of equipment. We are given five senses with which to see, hear, touch, smell, and taste our environment so that we may invest our belief in the validity of a dualistic external reality. Based on the appearance of form, separation from the whole looks, feels, and tastes real, even though it isn't.

Creating a body isn't enough. Our Spirit-Selves also need to create an environment upon which to experience a dualistic reality. We are energy and energy is everywhere. So, in order to disrupt the feeling of unity, create feelings of lack, and the appearance of a separate external reality, energy frequencies need to be filtered. The human body's energy field does this. It filters and processes particular frequencies through energy centers that are called chakras.

THE CHAKRAS

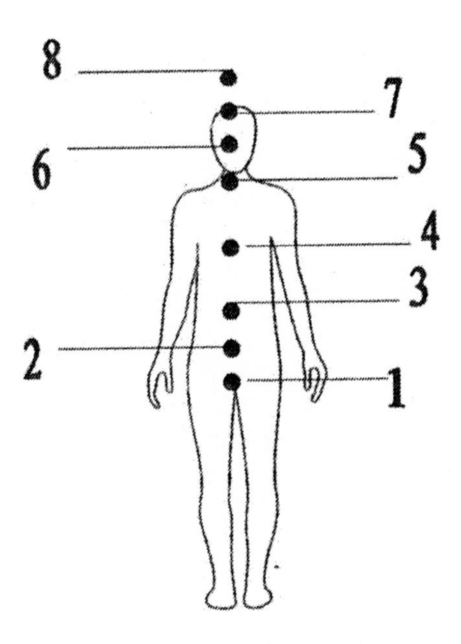

The chakras serve as revolving doors between the internal world and the external world. Each doorway handles a different frequency of energy according to its specific experiential purpose. Think of the physical, external world as a holodeck of projected energy that continuously flows out from the chakras onto an empty three-dimensional silver screen. The resulting projected reality in the external world will be due to the person's choice of either positive thought or negative thought in relation to the specific concepts being explored. Each projection from the “I Am” list will manifest into harmonious, peaceful, secure experiences. Each negative projection arising from the separate ego-self "I Am NOT" list will manifest in a negative experience or negative external environment. (See chapter 5 for chakra details).

What you think and believe is what you see, and what you see is what you get. What you get results in the confirmation of what you originally believed. Reality is a self-perpetuating mind game.

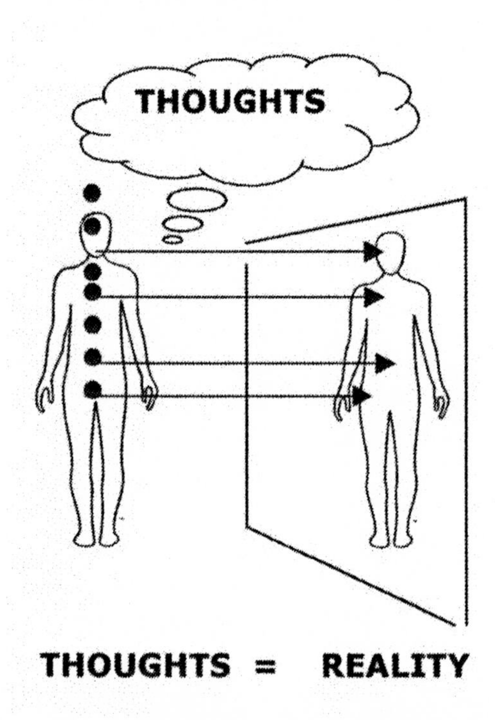

There is a constant barrage of opposing forces moving through us at all times, and it is imperative that we come to understand that we have the power to choose whether it will be the positive or the negative forces that will become the foundation of our individual illusionary reality. The roots of the creation of poverty, illness, and disease are found in the "NOTs" that are registered as blocks to the positive flow of energy in each person's energy field.

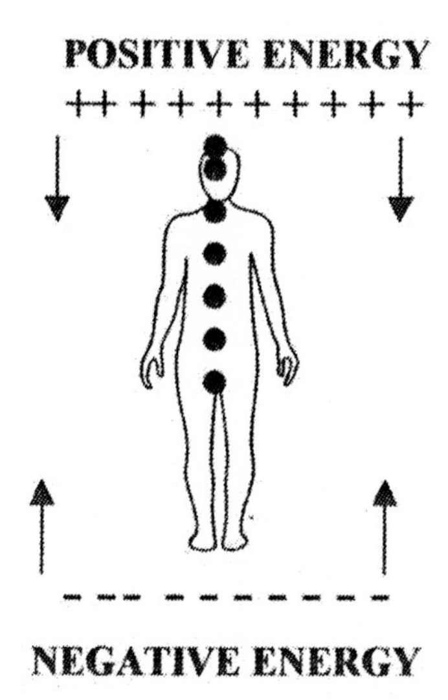

Its All Smoke and Mirrors:

There is nobody there but you.

Signs On Your Forehead

I have repeatedly stated that you and I are one. At this point it becomes important to understand that the energy of the whole spirit that we are communicates at every moment with the energy of the rest of the whole. This is the foundation of holistic health. Everything that is said and done reflects the connection between everything and everyone else that appears to be separate. Souls agree to participate in each other's personal reality creations. A block in the flow of energy in one's energy field serves as a teleprompter for all souls to read. Negative blocks that harbor our issues consist of thoughts, beliefs, and perceptions from the "I Am Not" list. They become reality as the surrounding people read and act out the script that each individual displays. Think of each negative or positive belief as a sign that you wear on your forehead. In this way judgments, limiting beliefs, and perceptions of lack repeat in your relationships until they are released. Patterns repeat because the signs remain the same. For example, if you feel like a powerless victim, the unconscious script assures that you will become one. If you want to change the pattern, then you must change the sign that you carry in your energy field.

Signs, Symbols and Synchronicity

Many of my clients have asked me the following question. My response is always the same.

Q. All my life I have prayed for a sign that I am on the right path, to no avail. I keep asking, but I never see a sign. Why is this?

A. Open your eyes. The signs are all around you.

Everything is screaming at you to put the pieces of the puzzle together. Absolutely nothing is separate or random. Nothing is unnecessary. We, together with every aspect of our lives, have an important interactive place in the universe. As I have said, the spiritual journey is a game, and we have left clues for ourselves all over the place. Who and what we are appears to us as a big puzzle where vignettes present themselves and need to be pasted together in the mind to complete the big picture. Energy is intelligent and singular. To say that there is instantaneous communication between parts of the energy would be incorrect because it is one whole unity. It is omnipotent because it is "All There Is."

One way to begin to recognize the unified connection of "All That Is," is by observing the dynamic flow of energy that runs between internal and external creations. Because the outside world will always reflect the personal internal world, we can see within our minds and hearts by reading these external reflections.

It is vital to understand that the horse goes before the cart. First the individual has the belief, thought or feeling, and then the external world mirrors the symbol as a reflection of the thought or feeling.

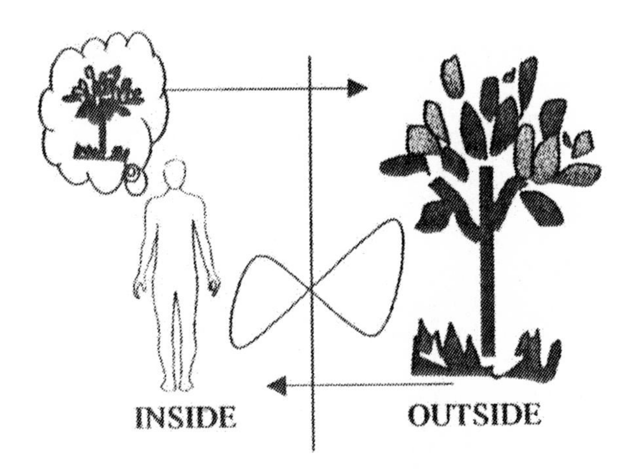

Early in my spiritual journey I began the process of becoming aware of my own personal external reflections. The labels in my clothes and shoes, the billboards that I frequently drove past, the names of the people that I dealt with, and even the large trucks that traveled next to me on the roadway, were all carrying reflective messages for me. They were neither coincidental flukes nor am I an egomaniac. My energy was, in fact, attracted to these messages to mirror my inner conflicts, challenges, and inherent solutions.

Back in the days of my confusion, my guides used to repeat to me over and over again, "God knows your name." I did not know what that meant then. When I began to connect the dots, I could see and appreciate a whole new level of being. Each moment, experience, place, and name are threads in the magnificent, brilliant weave of the fabric of life. Sometimes there are days and nights that I spend in heightened awareness. During these times, I can see the aspects of my personal net of gems. I am fortunate to be able to see the complex webs that connect us to our chosen lessons. The enormous amount of support and harmony available to every one of us is visible to me. I look forward to the days in the coming millennium when we are all able to look through the veils and see these hidden threads.

In the book *The Power of Myth with Bill Moyers,* Joseph Campbell refers to this phenomenon.

> "Shopenhauer, in his splendid essay called 'On an Apparent Intention in the Fate of the Individual, points out that when you reach an advanced age and look back over your lifetime, it can seem to have a consistent order and plan, as though composed by a novelist. Events that when they occurred had seemed accidental and of little moment turn out to have been indispensable factors in the composition of a consistent plot. So who composed that plot? Schopenhauer suggests that just as your dreams are composed by an aspect of yourself of which your consciousness is unaware, so too, your whole life is composed by the will within you. And just as people whom you will have met apparently by mere chance became leading agents in the structuring of your life, so, too, will you have served unknowingly as an agent, giving meaning to the lives of others. The whole thing gears together in one big symphony, with everything unconsciously structuring everything else. And Shoepenhauer concludes that it is as though our lives were the features of the one dream of a single dreamer in which all of the dream characters dream, too; so that everything links to everything else, moved by the one will to life which is the universal will in nature. It is a magnificent idea - an idea that appears in India in the mythic image of the Net of Indra, which is a net of gems, where at every crossing of one thread over another there is a gem reflecting all the other reflecting gems. Everything arises in mutual relation to everything else, so you can't blame anybody for anything."
>
> Joseph Campbell,
> *The Power of Myth with Bill Moyers*

I urge you to open up and begin to notice that you are the "All That Is" energy. Remove the blocks to your spirit self and you will be amazed at all the fascinating, creative ways that the universe is communicating with you. The following are some examples of how to read the external reflections.

I have a friend who constantly complains that the proprietor of her office does not keep the office clean. I recall her having the same complaint about the owners of the house where she used to live as a tenant. The real problem is that she is completely unaware of her need to clean the dust out of her energy field. She needs to get in touch with her feelings of jealousy, lack, limitation, resentment, and anger towards others. When my friend attends to cleaning the dust in her own interior, the proprietor will reflect her pristine energy pattern by providing a cleaner environment.

I remember having a colleague who felt a need to continually clean her mother's apartment whenever she visited. She repeatedly complained about how dirty and sloppy her mother 's apartment was. No matter how much she cleaned, when she returned it would be dirty again. Her mother was chronically ill with heart and lung problems, exhibited bi-polar behavior, and had been treated for a melanoma. There was a great deal of internal cleaning that needed to be done. The fact that her mother had ignored her issues of need and lack throughout her whole life showed up in her body's diseases as well as in her environmental surroundings.

Are your closets cluttered? Cluttered closets reflect a cluttered mind. Are your allergies acting up and causing you to use too many tissues? Tissues can be external representations of issues. The sound of a sneeze is very close to the sound of the word issue. Try getting in touch with your hidden feelings next time you are about to reach for a tissue. Do you have stacks and stacks of old magazine issues lying around? Chances are that old internal issues are not being processed and released.

LISTEN UP VETERINARIANS

Children and Animals

Children and animals can be our best teachers. Their jobs are to deliver supporting messages and images to us. On a soul level, they too read our energy scripts. I have a friend whose young son oversleeps so deeply that she has extreme difficulty waking him up for school. She is having a difficult time managing her financial responsibilities and is still undecided about a career course at the age of fifty. Her son is reflecting her resistance to waking up to her power to create her own happiness and abundance. She keeps missing her wake-up calls by looking for answers outside of herself.

Are your cats suffering from kidney problems? I have noticed that our wonderful animal friends are happy to join in the spirit game by relieving us of having to suffer the pains that accompany the messages sent to us from our unified energetic level of being. If your cats are having kidney problems, I suggest that you ask your kids if their needs are being met. (kid's needs = kidneys) Kids can also refer to your inner children.

Do you have a dog with hip dysplasia? Just the other day I made an inquiry as to how a client's baby cousin was doing. The baby had been born two years earlier with a severe hip problem. The condition was not diagnosed for the first year, even though it was evident that the baby's development was extremely slow. The baby was eventually fitted and treated with a brace. When I scanned the baby after birth, the guides pointed to the inner ear. My client answered my inquiry with, "Oh the baby is doing just fine now, but isn't it strange that the dog has developed a hip problem too?" Both the baby and the dog were signaling a balance problem within the family. Oh, did I forget to mention that the members of the family were religious extremists?

During a reading one day, a client's golden retriever puppy dog stood up on a chair and gave its owner a silent call for help. "Look," my client replied. "She is afraid to get down off the chair." I replied, "Look at your life right now. You are afraid to get up off the chair." A few months later, during another session, I saw the dog walking around with an empty baby bottle in its mouth. It was an absurd sight. There was no one in the family under sixteen years of age. The reading revealed that my client had been adopted as a baby and had harbored fears of abandonment throughout her life. She was still suffering from deep feelings of insecurity. The universal energy within her dog was signaling her that it was time for her to get in touch with her inner child. Her inner child needed re-assurance that she wasn't alone. She needed to feel safe. She needed to be encouraged to release the excessive fear.

When my son was three years old his favorite past time was to string yarn around furniture legs. He loved to tie knots in the yarn. Every day I would have to spend endless amounts of time untying the knots to remove the yarn. I now believe that his soul was trying to convey to me the profound truth that everything is connected. He was probably trying to mirror back to me the "NOTs" that were forming in my own energy field. These "NOTs" would later result in a massive energy crash.

Everything in the outside world is made up of energy that reads, communicates, assists, and harmonizes with our script. Personal reality is created in this way. We are only victims of our own psyche. We must come to understand that the universe serves as a mirror to reflect our own personal agendas back to us, not to victimize us, but rather to set us free from our unconscious self imposed chains. It is time to accept responsibility and give up the blame.

Chapter 3

Form Follows Function

Energy Function = to create personal reality with free will

There Is Nobody Here But You And Your Reflection

> "Reality is what we take to be true. What we take to be true is what we believe. What we believe is based upon our perceptions. What we perceive depends upon what we look for. What we look for depends upon what we think. What we think depends upon what we perceive. What we perceive determines what we believe. What we believe determines what we take to be true. What we take to be true is our reality."
>
> Gary Zukov, *The Dancing Wu Li Masters*

Nothing Comes Into Your Life Uninvited

We are shape shifters. We are the creators of our reality, as well as an intrinsic part of it. We are using this awesome creative power at every moment. Most of the time, however, we are unaware that we are using it and how we are using it.

If I were to show a homemade video to a primitive tribe, they might think of me as an evil spirit using a form of magic to capture tribal members in a box. Photography, however, is not magic, but rather the result of an integrated set of orderly principles of light. The people would not be in the box, only their light reflections would be. The manufacturing and use of the equipment would be based on the principles of cause and effect; when they are used in a given way, particular results would be achieved. Intentional use of the equipment would produce the desired images. This is also the case with our experiential reality. On the surface we may understand cause and effect as it applies to behavior, however, there is also an underlying order to the movement of energy and the resulting manifestation of form. The more that we learn about this invisible order, the more power we have to influence creation.

Energy acts according to particular laws of motion. Just as the physical plane has Newton's laws of motion and gravity, the subatomic realm comes with its own set of principles. Energy is perpetually arranging and rearranging itself according to the following rules.

The Law of Abundance - That which is multiples.

The Law of Attraction - Like attracts like.

The Law of Balance – Energy seeks balance. Dynamic energy moves toward equilibrium.

The first law of energy is the **Law of Abundance.** This law states that everything that you see and focus on will multiply. Have you ever noticed a particular kind of car that you have never seen before, and then from the time that you became aware of it, you began to see it everywhere? This is how the Law of Abundance works. According to the law, whatever you see, you will see more of. If you see lack, there will be more lack appearing. If you see yourself as poor, you will see more poverty. If you feel disabled, you will see more disability. If you see yourself as rich, you will get richer. If you see yourself as weak, you will feel weaker. If you see yourself as a victim, there will be more victim situations arising.

The second law is the **Law of Attraction.** This law states that like attracts like. This means that energy will attract more of its particular kind of energy to itself. For example, if you are a liberal thinker, you will attract liberal thinkers. If you are a positive person, you will attract positive people and events to you. Respectively, if you choose to be a negative thinker, you will attract more negative people and events to you. Victims bond with victims. People who feel successful have successful friends. People who are timid and fearful attract more of the same. That which comes into your life enters with an invitation presented by the energy that you carry.

The third law is the **Law of Balance.** This law states that energy seeks balance, and that dynamic energy seeks equilibrium. The law explains the cause and direction of the movement of energy. Just as a seesaw moves up and down based on the amount of pressure applied to either end, energy flows according to the amount of positive and negative charge that it acquires. In its natural state, energy will seek equilibrium by moving to balance its positive and negative charge. For example, in the following diagram, if the man were to step off of the negative side of the lever, (release his hold on predominantly negative thoughts) the lever would spring back to a horizontal, neutral position of balance.

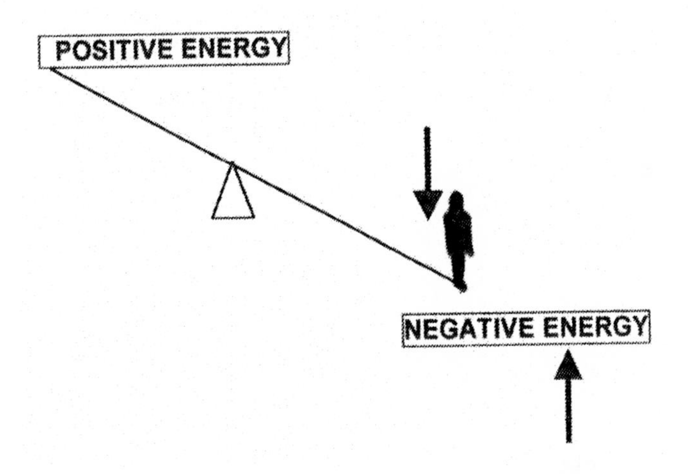

When a pendulum swings all the way to the left, it returns to swing an equal distance to the right. When it runs out of dynamic energy it will stop moving and remain vertically balanced between the right and the left side, until a new pressure is applied in either direction.

Now visualize a dualistic horizontal line with one end representing your internal thought energy and the other end representing the energy of the external physical world. What exists inside will automatically seek external balance by finding its existence in a physical reality.

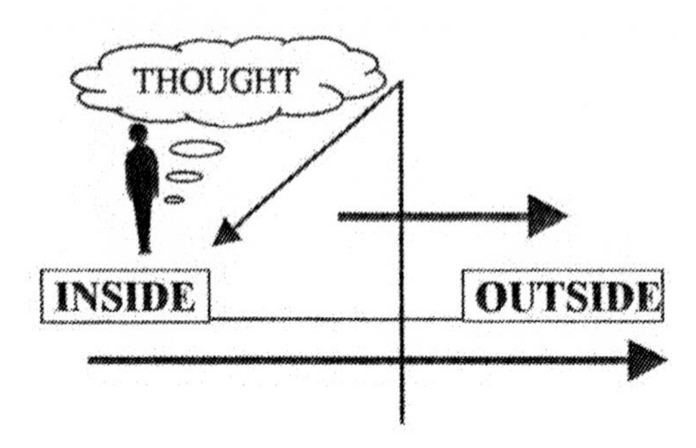

THOUGHT ENERGY MOVES TO MANIFEST YOUR PERSONAL REALITY

This explains why it is so important to recognize, process, and release our worries and fears. Visualization is a powerful tool of creation. It will produce that which we desire as well as that which we fear. Unless we manufacture a thought block, a negation of the original thought to counteract its power, the original thought will manifest externally. This is how thoughts and ideas become reality. The outside world will always reflect your personal, internal world. We, as creators, unknowingly breathe life into our thoughts. We give active power to ideas. When we add emotion to our thoughts, we give them an additional boost to manifest more rapidly as our reality.

Why We Don't Get What We Want?

So why don't all of our thoughts manifest? They don't all become real because we have thousands of thoughts every minute, and we don't stay with most of them long enough for them to build up enough energy to manifest. Sometimes we cancel out a positive thought with a negative thought.

Winning the lottery is a good example of a thought that many people would like to see manifest. However, along with this desire, we have many counteractive thoughts that abort the physical manifestation of the thought. For example, we have thoughts that we do NOT deserve to win, thoughts that we are NOT worthy of having a lot of money, thoughts that money is the root of all evil, thoughts that winning would be too good to be true, and we have thoughts containing fear of change and responsibility. In addition, we carry many thoughts of limitation about the way that the world works. When we deny our belief in the power of internal creation, we abort the immediate power connected to the movement of energy toward the production of our desires. Jesus could manifest instantaneously because of his ability to see and understand the power of universal unity. With his strong belief in this power and without the creation of negative thought blocks in his field, his visions could quickly and easily become physical reality.

Conflicts in the Energy Field

When a person believes that he lacks the power to create the circumstances of his life, he is carrying victim consciousness. Negatively charged thoughts draw negative circumstances to the person who holds this kind of negative belief system. The result is that the person becomes immersed in a reality that confirms a state of powerlessness, lack, and need. However, the person holding victim consciousness does not see or believe that his own choice of thought is connected to the resulting experience.

For example, if a person fears NOT having enough money or security, then that will be the subsequent reality that is created. The person will then feel like a victim of external circumstances. On the other hand, if a person sees an abundant world, feels deserving, and desires something that he focuses on, he will receive in the external world that which he desires and more. One must positively believe in abundance for it to become his or her reality.

We have the power to choose thoughts with a positive or negative magnetic charge. Sometimes, however, we invoke conflicting thoughts containing both positive and negative energy. A person may want something, create a thought or vision energetically, but NOT feel deserving or good enough about himself to do what it takes to attain that which he wants. For example, he might desire to become a doctor, but NOT feel smart enough. Then obstacles will manifest as experiences that show him that he is NOT smart enough. Perhaps he will fail an entry exam. The external world will always confirm core personal beliefs, because internal energy is projected onto the external screen called the outside world. You are blueprinting for your reality at all times.

Returning to the example above, maybe this person feels smart enough to become a doctor, but believes that it takes a lot of money that he does NOT have. This kind of thinking gives power to the perspective of lack.

Consequently, he will meet with blocks to his desires. In the reverse, even if this person is not very smart or rich, but if he believes in himself, his abilities, and his worth, the external energy will manifest according to his desires because they will be supported by his build up and projection of positive energy. Perhaps he will apply for and receive a scholarship.

Universal energy manifests according to all thought requests, whether they carry a positive or negative charge. Whenever there is a passion in the heart for something, energy manifests a path toward it. However, even though the path may be there, it may be full of obstacles created by the core negative thoughts and beliefs stated in the ego-self "I am NOT" list. These blocks need to be cleared for the person to realize the existence of the path.

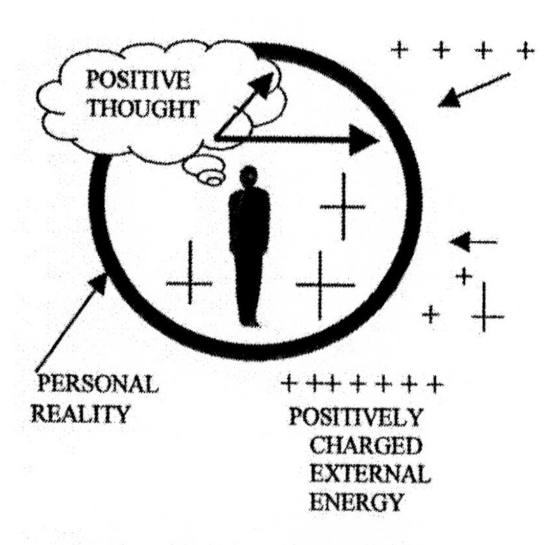

THE LAW OF ATTRACTION

Guilt

The most prevalent and powerful hidden negative energy, aside from fear, which underlies our manifestations and kills the physical realization of our true hearts desire, is guilt. Some of our cultural and religious history has given us the belief that "desire" is just a bad thing. So, every time a desire is formed, it is accompanied by guilt. The notion that poverty and lack of material gain are spiritual assets is a popular guilt generator. Even when they are not expressed, these negative beliefs get passed along to us in religious undertones. Guilt blocks feelings of self worth. It is stored in the solar plexus area and is the most difficult energy to apprehend and clear. It is no wonder that we have a hard time watching a positive thought manifest. Conflicting thoughts are so ubiquitous that we are constantly getting in our own way. That is why we don't get what we truly want.

LISTEN UP DOCTORS AND CHIROPRACTORS; THERE IS MORE TO HEALING THAN FIXING THE PHYSICAL PROBLEM.

The body is a mirror for consciousness. It has the capacity to appear perfect, if that is what the external reflection requires according to internal design.

Energy Field Health Scans

In the course of my work as an intuitive, I am often asked to comment on the state of a person's health. To do that I must examine the person's energy field where I can read the causal layers of energy that are the blueprint of a personal reality, according to current and past thoughts, beliefs, and perceptions. This is accomplished by asking the spirit guides to activate an energy field scan where I watch a horizontal bar move slowly down over the body's energy field. I observe by watching my inner visual screen, rather than the person's actual body. Because the smooth flow of energy throughout the energy field fuels the creation of health, when there is negative energy blocking the positive flow of energy in the system, the restriction will light up to signal me of its existence. In my inner vision, the scan resembles a radar screen. When I focus on the restriction, I can read the energy to determine where it came from and what it's purpose is. Restrictions will relate to past or present issues on the "I Am NOT" list.

Every time there is a perception of a hurtful trauma involving lack or loss, negative thoughts, feelings, and beliefs are initiated and an imperceptible dark spot is formed on the energy field. Each of these dark spots contains a negative magnetic charge and will attract similar negative perceptions and events to the person, according to the laws of attraction and multiplication. Every succeeding negative thought or feeling regarding that event adds additional dots in and around the first. These additional dots cluster to form what appears to be a dark cloud of dust in the energy field. When energy field dust is left unattended, it affects the person's future events, perceptions, and feelings. The larger or denser the dust cloud gets, the more power it has to attract more negativity into the person's life.

Negative energy registers on the energy field as a small vortex, which emits a negative charge. These vortices absorb surrounding positive energy, leaving less energy available to the individual for positive creative use. The slang for a negative energy vortex is an energy leak. An unprocessed negative feeling or perspective is like a dangling sentence. It has not completed its journey home to truth and fullness. Its completion requires seeing it in its larger context and attaching it to its missing positive aspects. When this occurs, the negative energy is reversed, and the spots are automatically cleared.

When I scan an adult energy field, I often find dark clouds of dust attributed to an emotional wound sustained in childhood. I have observed that part of the inner child splinters off and feels frightened, rejected, confused, alone, and powerless. It separates itself from the rest of the person, as if it were hiding in a closet. There it sits, stuck in another time frame, alone and terrified until someone comes along, opens the door, throws on the light, and assures it that the monster is gone, and that it will be loved and protected.

The initial wound in the fragmented child is often accompanied by an energy restriction in the throat chakra because the repressed need to communicate, cry or scream is often a contributing factor to the trauma. The adult is usually aware of this feeling of restriction, but hasn't any idea as to why it exists.

When a person holds onto negative energy, it is because at a deep level a choice is being made to continue to manifest and experience the negative side of duality. Understanding the original cause of darkness is not enough, in and of itself, to bring about a healing. Insight is the foundation for initiating the healing process. Discovering the negative energy gives us the power to make a choice to immediately release and replace it with positive energy, rather than to wait for the energy to naturally shift into balance and completion in its own time.

However, when a wounded inner child is holding onto the negativity, it is the spirit of the splintered off child, not the adult, that needs to express, release, and participate in positive replacement healing work before it will agree to integrate and feel whole again. An inner child splinter exerts a great deal of control over our emotions and behaviors. It is very difficult to heal this part of ourselves. To heal the splintered child we must travel back in time to the original source of the problem.

In a normal state of consciousness only the adult can be directly addressed. This is why so many clients complain that they have spent years in therapy doing inner child work, but say that they do not see any visible change for the better in their lives. Talking about the inner child is not the same as traveling through the time dimension and working directly with the young, splintered off spirit. Wounded inner child healing work can be done in a deep meditative state or hypnotic state. In these altered states of mind we have the ability to travel through the time dimension and effect change in the actual childhood spirit.

Although many deep wounds originate in childhood, an area of darkness can arise at any time in life and build into a negative energy cloud. A cloud constructed out of guilt is a call by the subconscious for constant self-punishment, sabotage, and victimization, all of which contribute to feelings of lack of power and create even more darkness. And so it goes, round and round. Worry and fear are the classic causes of adult energy leaks that precipitate disease. Doctors call them stress.

Cancer is the disease of unfinished business. Many unresolved forgiveness issues usually accompany it. Blame, self-judgment, jealousy, lack of power, and self pity are some additional triggers that activate negative energy clusters. Anger, grief, and resentment, are common examples of emotions that are stuffed inside and remain unexpressed and unprocessed. Sometimes people are taught by their tribe that silence is golden. Sometimes they are afraid that if they express their true feelings they will be rejected. Fear of abandonment is an insidious and powerful reason to hold back the spoken word. Processing feelings of anger, fear, and grief can be painful. When we get stuck in issues from the "I Am NOT" list and can't seem to find our way back to the "I AM" list, clouds of dust remain on the field, actively working to create illness and disease.

When energy clouds form, the spirit is sending a message to the body to ring an alarm to alert us to finish processing the stagnant emotional energy. The body responds with some form of illness as a way of saying, "Hey you, put your attention here. You need to make some kind of change in perception, attitude or belief to realign with truth." When a change in thought is made which allows the energy to flow freely again, the root purpose for the illness is nullified and permanent healing results.

When clouds build up, eventually enough negativity is drawn in and enough turmoil produced that the individual will develop a willingness to let go of the negative patterns and rethink values, priorities, habits, and choices. This is known as the classic wake up call. There are however, other alternatives to effect a timelier, gentler healing. (See Chapter 7, Healing Methods and Therapies).

It should also be mentioned that a chemical or surgical healing will not heal an energy vortex. If the issues of the unfinished business are not addressed during the period of illness or recovery, then after the original illness is fixed, another illness will rear its ugly head. Discomfort of some sort will continue until a wake up call illness arises, or until some form of healing is initiated to expose, process, and release the negative energy root. Sometimes just having a realization of the need for change and an intention to release the negative energy will magnetize healing to an individual. At other times some assistance is called for, and the client may wish to seek an appropriate holistic healer to facilitate the healing process. I advise caution and discernment in making the choice of a facilitator.

Holistic Healers

It seems in vogue these days for traditional health practitioners to refer to themselves as holistic healers. "Holistic," when attached to a medical practitioner's name, can be a misleading, commercial mask. This title has brought a prevailing, but too superficial, misunderstanding to the community that the word holistic means respect for the trinity of body, mind, and spirit, as three separate aspects of the self. This meaning, however widely used, is misleading.

The word holistic actually carries with it the understanding that, mind, body, and spirit are ONE single expression. What appears to be the problem in the physical body is really just a physical signal that there is a negative energy cloud lodged on the energy field that is blocking the creation of health and happiness. "Holistic" means that the body is expressing the spirit. It implies the recognition of a causal connection between feeling, thought, perception, and the manifestation of physical reality.

When the body manifests illness, it is helping you to discover that you have invested your energy in a dualistic, negative choice. It is validating your creative power by helping you to remember who you really are as a unified, creator God-Self. In this way illness serves as a stepping-stone on the spiritual journey.

Fixing the body without picking up the message containing the purpose for the illness can challenge the body to turn up the volume in its own physical language of pain. A holistic healer recognizes that a physical problem in the body is a signal that the person needs change, clearing, and balance in one's life. Restrictions in the energy field show themselves in physical form in unlimited creative ways. Therefore, a true holistic healer recognizes that fixing the body is not the entire goal, but rather a partial solution to a larger process.

Sincere holistic healers will recognize that their job is to facilitate the client in any of the following four steps towards healing. The first step is the recognition and identification of the negative energy. If we are to heal, we must begin to see the aspect of the illusion that is being experienced as a part of the larger human experience that contains a positive purpose. Affirming that one has the innate power to change is the second step. Sincere intention to release the negative energy is the third step. Following through with positive change and balance is the fourth step on the healing path.

Energy Crash

Many people who seek holistic healers are experiencing an excessive build up of negative energy. Some of my new clients are people who are experiencing the effects of being at the core of a negative energy spiral. Their lives appear to be falling apart. Finances, relationships, and bodies accelerate breakdown procedures when the person's negative energy charge grows proportionately greater than the personal stock of positive energy because positive energy fuels the creation of health and happiness. The more that goes wrong, the more that one focuses on what appears to be missing in one's life. As perceptions of lack grow, so do feelings that reality does not contain whatever it takes to fulfill one's needs and desires. As perceptions feed feelings and feelings feed perceptions, negative manifestations multiply until the person has exhausted the conventional means of assistance and support including doctors, therapists, psychiatrists, friends, relatives, and financial counselors. That is when the angels guide my clients to call me to connect them to their spirit guides.

HOLDING ON TO TOO MUCH NEGATIVE ENERGY CAUSES AN ENERGY CRASH.

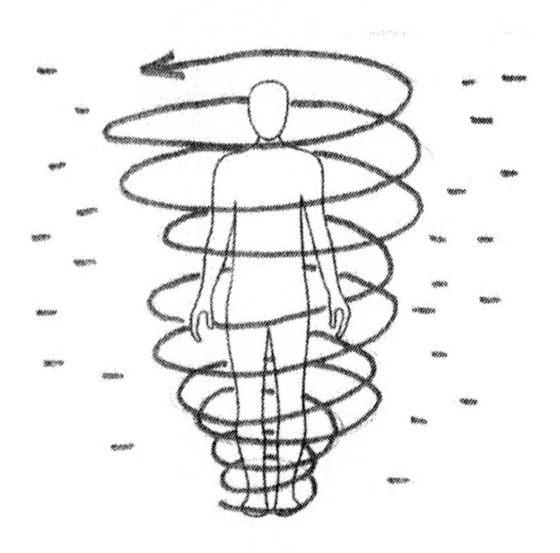

NEGATIVELY CHARGED ENERGY FIELD CRASH

I am grateful and fortunate to hear from my clients just when they have decided that something needs to change. When a "dark night of the soul" experience happens, the light begins to dawn on them that they had better listen up and embrace a new personal agenda. A dark night experience doesn't happen by accident. It happens because they allow their lives to proceed without making the necessary course corrections that would create happiness and well-being. I explain to my clients how their free will choices are burying them with every negative thought and feeling that they are having. In order to change one's emotional energetic charge, one must make the necessary, positive changes to one's life as well as to one's choice of thoughts and belief systems. The changes must allow for the alignment of one's heart's desires with one's will.

A negative energy spiral is the equivalent of being within an invisible tornado that destroys all aspects of your life. A positive spiral will move in the opposite direction. A good, strong, positive energy spiral will manifest heaven on earth so that life takes on a joyful, magical feeling.

Chapter 4

Energy is Power

Think for yourself: Hold on to your power.

Group energy desires that you conform and assign your personal power of choice to the group dogma. However, when an individual automatically accepts opinions, judgments, thoughts, and beliefs from another person or group, without knowing why that he does, he gives his power of choice away in an effort to shirk his personal responsibility to think and choose for himself.

We all have the ability to access an abundance of energy to create whatever it is that we choose to experience while in our human body. However, when we as adults blindly accept another's thoughts and beliefs, without making a conscious choice to do so, we use our energy to create that person's or the group's creation in place of our own. It is sometimes simply easier to go along with others, rather than to put energy into creating a personal menu of choices and make personal decisions. Lack of confidence and fear of failure can cause us to shirk this personal responsibility.

Because we own our power, we have the right to give it away, if we choose to do so. People, who hold on to negative self worth issues, often give their power away by agreeing with group dogma in exchange for feelings of love and acceptance. This is essentially the act of selling one's soul. Acquiescing to a group mind out of a feeling of guilt, rather than conviction is the same thing. While joining a group mind can feel like a temporary solution to feelings of lack of power and self-validation, it can also serve to mask the individual work that needs to be done to guide an individual to develop feelings of self-love and integrity.

Everything in our society says, "Let me think for you." We are spoon fed our thoughts and belief systems by groups, institutions, and organizations that want us to add our energy to their collective agenda. Political parties, the medical community, insurance brokers, corporations, institutions, unions, and organized religions are all examples of group energies that advocate their group's agenda. The more people who join in the group belief, the more powerful the group feels. People who do NOT acknowledge their personal power join groups to increase their clout. Politicians know that many of their constituents prefer NOT to think for themselves. They use this fact when they advertise their polling results to convince you to vote for them merely because others are doing so.

As a society, we allow our commercial entities to invade and exploit our thought processes with a continuous barrage of fear statements that bombard our minds with messages that tell us what we need and who we should be. The diet industry thrives on our low self-esteem. The insurance industry constantly reminds us of our fears of loss and death. The fashion industry reinforces our need for validation. It would be wise to take our personal power back from the large corporations whose sole interests lie in the amount of income that they can generate from us.

When a person chooses, either consciously or unconsciously, to allow others to create belief systems for him or her, that person takes on the role of a victim in an accidental world. Exercising your power to choose your own thoughts allows you to recognize the connection between thought causes and experiential effects. This correlation is vital to developing an understanding of your personal part in creation. Making conscious "thought" choices and increasing our awareness of our underlying beliefs are necessary for the recognition of conscious creation. We must begin to pay attention to our own thoughts and the resulting pictures of reality. It is time to learn how to connect the dots. When we do, we will learn to see that perceptions of lack begets more lack, abundant thinking brings abundance, and positive perspective brings joy. It is time to recognize and to let go of the false security offered by group energy. Tribal energy can rob you of your individual power of choice that underlies the creation of your health and happiness.

We need to teach our children to develop more faith in their inner God-Self. We need to encourage them to think and make individual choices, rather than to simply obey and accept choices that are made for them. Soul maturity requires independent thinking. Independent thinking leads to self-respect and self-love. It is the doorway back to the God-Self.

The movie *Twelve Angry Men* discloses the huge effort that is required in examining one's own mind in relation to complex situations. The movie shows the work involved in making responsible decisions, rather than taking the easy way out by thoughtlessly joining in with the group's choice.

In The Name of Love

Adopting the group agenda can feel like a curse when the tribe contains negative or limiting belief systems, and it can feel like a blessing when the tribe is graced with an abundance of positive energy. Investing energy in tribal beliefs can hold you to limitation and fear. Romeo and Juliet are classic examples of the painful conflict that one can feel when having to choose between loyalties to the tribe or to one's own heart. It is not unusual for a group agenda to require self-sacrifice. The need for sacrifice produces a power play between the tribe and the self. Rules and regulations of clubs and religions can present these kinds of fearful internal conflicts.

Many blocks that arise in the chakras are the result of family imprinting. When this is the case, it becomes your life's work to take each one of the negative beliefs, attitudes, and perspectives that are adopted from the tribe, and turn them around so that you may experience the positive energy that results from making new and different positive choices. Often, it is necessary to have to experience the effects of your negative beliefs and expectations in the way of an external disruption before you can recognize that something within you needs to change. This is called a wake-up call. It is a signal to weed out negative, fearful, and limiting thoughts, beliefs, attitudes, and actions, and replace them with ones that lead to a more fulfilling personal reality.

Rejecting the family agenda requires that you pull your roots out from the tribal mind. This can be very difficult and painful. If the individual has not developed a solid sense of self-support and validation, then it can feel like an impossible task.

Family energy can share common beliefs that underlie the creation of health and illness. Sometimes family members unknowingly choose to invest their energy in particular diseases. Cancer and heart disease are just two examples where the medical community tells family members that they are in a genetic high-risk group. But, are these diseases a product of our genetic heredity, or are they the result of thought and behavior patterns that are passed down through the generations? Creating the very same behavior patterns, fears, beliefs, perceptions, and expectations as our ancestors did can produce identical results.

My readings indicate that heart disease is common in men who opt for the dysfunctional pattern of shutting down their heart chakras. Men in our society are taught NOT to feel and express their emotions. Heart disease may be the result of faulty inherited eating habits, but the root cause of eating unhealthy foods can be the negative energy emitted from the heart chakra. This creates a desire for those unhealthy fatty foods so that the body can produce a physical signal that something is amiss in that area. Cancer is a symptom of massive energy blocks, many of which come from thought patterns and imbalances that are passed from one generation to the next.

Sometimes a person will be able to see dysfunctional behavior within the family and reject the harmful pattern, but will not follow through with the release of blame that came from having previously adopted the group pattern. In order to heal, one must complete the resolution of unfinished business by pulling one's focus of energy out of the painful past. A lack of forgiveness can lead a person to become that which he chooses to judge because the judgmental energy will clone the dysfunctional situation due to the Laws of Attraction and Multiplication. This is often the case with family behavior patterns of abuse and addiction.

Looking Back

Be careful. When negative memories containing victim situations are replayed in the mind along with a plethora of negative emotions such as fear, anger, blame, confusion, resentment, and betrayal, the memories become present visualizations. These are then propelled into manifestation by the strength of the emotions connected to them.

The Now - Moment

The power to create is vested in every now-moment. Each individual has the choice to invest the focus of his or her energy in reliving moments of the past or in creating a desired future. We choose that which appears to offer us the best payoff. If we enjoy wallowing in sympathy, then we will replay in our mind our entire victim script from the past. This will automatically bring on more of the same. If we are lazy and fearful, we might choose to create disease merely to escape the work of creating a satisfying life. If we seek attention, we might create a variety of illnesses that help us to gather lots of loving attention from friends, family and health care practitioners. If, on the other hand, we value life for its opportunities, challenges, and adventures, then we can have fun playing with the creative opportunities that we draw into our lives.

Each one of us has the power to create whatever provides the most happiness. Look at the life that you have created. Ask yourself to identify the payoffs in each area of your life. If you don't like what you see, you have the power to decide to break out of your pattern and make a change.

Is fear of the unknown keeping you glued to a dull, unsatisfying life? Are you merely resolved to living the patterns of your life because that is the way generations of your ancestors did? Do you use your perception of lack of money as an excuse to accept rather than create? Are you just dying to make changes, but afraid to? The power to release the fear and replace it with courage can be a decision away. What dreams have you been putting off for some day? The now-moment offers a new beginning in every moment of every day of your life.

To do a now-moment reality check, ask yourself, "Are you where you want to be, doing what you want to be doing, right now?" If not, it may be time to look at your excuses and reevaluate to what, and whom, you have assigned your power. With focus, clear intention, and effort, we all have the opportunity to begin to rearrange the options available to us in every moment. Your creative Spirit-Self reaction to these thoughts will be, "Let's get to work creating something new." Your negative ego-self will say, "You're crazy. It's impossible."

In The Fullness of Time

It is the nature of the human journey to experience both sides of many dualistic equations such as poverty, wealth, sickness, and health. These are the elements in our soul contract. Perhaps when we get tired of being the victim, we decide to come back to earth to experience being a rescuer or a hero. Perhaps when we tire of being the nun, we decide to come back as a prostitute. When playing the part of the hero gets boring, maybe we create a bad guy role. Be assured that the act of judging a particular role sets us up to audition for that part. There is no perfect part. Each role teaches us more about what it means to be human.

Karma

When we create karma, we leave a piece of ourselves attached to the negative past. This missing piece calls out to us to be retrieved. Time offers a field of opportunity for that missing piece to be integrated. The Law of Balance spans our entire soul history. Therefore, the completion process may require one lifetime or many.

Karma can be the reason why we come into a particular family. Family imprinting can be a powerful tool that sets us up for the experiences that we need to have in order to find completion. The system is perfect because it is based on the past conscious choices of each soul. It offers each soul new opportunities to change perceptions and choices. There is an underlying purpose to this apparent madness. When karmic lessons are complete, power is restored and we feel whole again.

Judgment, blame, and guilt are the basic negative energies of unfinished business that deposit dust in the energy field. When dust is created, it must eventually be cleaned up.

When we do not forgive another, we hold a vision of the aspect of that other person that we judge and eventually manifest it within ourselves. In other words, we become the aspect of the person that we do not forgive. That is why child victims often become adult victimizers.

At the end of the day, all negative energy must find its way home to a positive perspective. After all, if there is nobody there but one whole spirit being, then there is nobody to judge, blame, or forgive. If you believe that you are the creator of your own experience, then you must acknowledge that although others appear to take part in a conspiracy to hurt or betray you, in accordance with your script, they are really only helping you to get you where you need to go, by your higher design. Remember, nothing comes into your life uninvited. Therefore, knowing that you are the one that is responsible for the experience, you must retract your negative energy. This is forgiveness.

Contrary to popular understanding, forgiveness does not mean that you choose to forget about the behavior of another because an event happened in the past. True forgiveness means that you recognize that judgment doesn't have any positive purpose and will seed an abundance of negative energy within you. Forgiveness requires a conscious choice not to use your power to create negative energy. Judgment registers blocks in the energy field and attracts additional negative experience until it is cleared. Judgment and blame must be released for true forgiveness to occur. This is part of the victim lesson. Retracting your own negative energy immediately clears the dust accumulated and opens up the flow of positive energy. This is the healing path.

When we blame another, we ignite a deep-seated feeling of guilt within us because our Spirit-Self knows that there is no one else responsible for creating our own personal reality. However, accepting responsibility for energetic participation in the creation of the event does not exclusively dissolve the guilt. In fact, it can cause a substantial increase in feelings of guilt, which produces an energetic call for self-punishment. Guilt can only be released by retracting both the original blame assigned to the other person and the underlying self-judgment.

Feeling Tired? Are You Low on Energy?

The body needs positive energy to create health and the psyche needs positive energy to create satisfying, fulfilling feelings of happiness and joy. We all know the tired feeling that results when we are running on low energy. That feeling comes about from the following three possible causes. We feel tired when:

1. we need rest and renewal.

2. the positive flow of energy through the chakras is restricted and blocked by negative energy vortices. These vortices are little black holes through which positive energy leaks. When energy leaks, we lose power.

3. positive energy drains through a cord connected to another person. This is how we give our power away.

The following information will describe how and why many of us feel so tired due to #2 and #3

Energy Vampires

Negative energy vortices are exhausting to house. Think of energy vortices as little black holes that pull in everything around them. They not only eat up the positive energy leaving the owner feeling tired, but they also drain the energy from the people that they come in contact with.

A sufficient supply of positive energy is needed to function. When the positive flow of energy within us is blocked, we sense that something is missing. We feel tired. If this goes on for an extended time, we get depressed and frustrated. When people create an excess of negative energy, due to perceptions of lack and fear, they are forced to search outside of themselves to fill up their emptiness. Negative energy addicts turn into energy vampires to replenish their constantly diminishing supply.

Gnawing feelings of something missing can create a perpetual state of neediness in the energy vampire. In the energy vampire, the need for validation reaches astronomical levels. Energy vampires will constantly seek validation of their action, opinion, appearance, talent, intelligence, and importance. They demand time and attention from others to feed the positive feelings of power that they cannot sustain independently. They exhibit a constant need to be right. Low self-esteem escalates judgment, blame, and victim thinking. The vampire's perpetual creation of negative energy causes loss of more and more available physical energy. When more energy is lost, more is needed to function and feel comfortable.

The severe energetic depletion of the energy vampire leads to an unending call for attention from others. But, trying to fill a vampire's needs is like trying to fill a bottomless pit. Although a vampire may be a family member that you love and want to help, you cannot satisfy the vampire's hunger. Attempting to fill the vampire's needs will only serve to bring the vampire back for more energy and leave you feeling totally exhausted. Vampires must learn to support their own energy bank by filling up with energy from the internal connection to the God-Self, rather than draining energy from others. You cannot help them by giving constant attention and validation. You can help them by providing the truth about their appetite for negative energy. This is the case with alcoholic addiction. The reason that the twelve step programs are so effective is because they teach the importance of reconnecting with one's internal spiritual foundation.

Poor Me

One tool of the Energy Vampires is the "poor me" syndrome. The message here is, "Feel sorry for me." This is a way to elicit someone's time and attention. People who like to make a habit of dumping their troubles onto others without making concerted efforts towards finding solutions and making changes, get an energy high from sympathy, which is an affirmation of their lack of power to change their circumstances. Energy vampires aren't looking for solutions. They are seeking your energy.

You can tell when you are talking to vampires because they will always run from the light. When you affirm that he has the power to create change, the vampire will often get angry and attack with the ego-self. He will aim for an emotional reaction from you that will emit energy back to him. Energy vampire's love to complain and to argue. A strong negative emotional reaction from you is a vampire's dream comes true. Do not be fooled. You do NOT help a vampire when you give away your energy. You only satisfy an unhealthy addiction and drain yourself. Are there people in your life now that always seem to leave you feeling tired and drained?

Cords

A healthy, well-balanced individual will use his power to manifest his desired goals. This person will find joy in using his creative juices. However, someone who doesn't understand the value of his creative energy will often choose to give his personal power away to another. By doing this, this person is enlisting the assistance of another individual to help him to discover his underlying negative feelings.

When two souls agree to interact and play out their feelings of lack, they form a cord between them that houses their negative energy. The negative energy comes from the agreed upon false beliefs from the "I Am NOT" list. A cord is a very real phenomenon in the spirit realm. It serves a purpose. The cord will relay energy between the two parties. It will keep two people tied together. Each one will feed the other's issues of lack, until one decides to break free from the negative self-perception.

Two people that are connected to a negative energy cord are doing a dance. An action by one will cause a reaction in the other. When a negative pattern is recognized, the person who chooses to remove the veil of innocence and see the true issue, may cut the cord in a meditative state. This will help the person to process the lesson more rapidly. When the lessons are learned naturally, healthy positive energy is restored, and the cords are automatically discarded.

Sometimes people get stuck in the dance for very long periods of time. Without realizing it they will go round and round, perpetually repeating the dynamic, negative energy pattern. These patterns get moved along from one generation to another. This is called inherited karma.

Victims and Abusers

VICTIM ———————— **ABUSER**

VICTIMS AND VICTIMIZERS SHARE A NEGATIVE ENERGY CORD

The Law of Attraction will assure that victims and victimizers have innate radar that attracts them to each other. They represent both sides of a victimization experience. Giving and receiving abuse are manifestations of feelings of lack of power and self worth. Cords connect these two souls together to play out their matching issues.

Both victims and abusers hold on to feelings of lack. Abusers seek emotional reactions to gain feelings of power.

When an emotional reaction is sought, but not produced, the abuser will usually yank harder on the cord by increasing the abuse as a way of demanding an emotional reaction. Abusers will belittle, degrade, scare, confuse, create crisis, criticize, rage, whine or even cry, seeking reactions such as anger, guilt, fear, and pity in an effort to feel the power to exert control over another. The victim's reactions will provide a temporary energy boost for the abuser, and will be a confirmation of the lack of power of the victim.

Victims and abusers hold on to feelings of anger and fear. Each one is mirroring the other's emotions. The abuser is reflecting the victim's repressed anger. The victim is mirroring the abuser's low self-esteem. Sometimes there isn't any awareness of the emotions that are being stockpiled. But, energy is impersonal. It doesn't care if one is aware or not. It does its job according to its own principles. When emotional energy accumulates in excessive amounts, the abuser becomes explosive.

PASSIVE ———————— **AGGRESSIVE**

Passive-aggressive behavior is another example of an energy dynamic between two individuals that share a negative energy cord. When a person whose energy script reads, "Allow me to create for you," meets and dances with "Do it for me," a soul agreement is forged whereby a co-dependent relationship is established.

Those that invite others to create their lives for them give up the ability to learn from trial and error. The act of giving one's power of choice away to another is an escape from taking responsibility for one's happiness. When life does not go the way they would like, they perceive themselves as victims. This kind of relationship creates a ripe energy dynamic for the formulation of blame. This is the foundation of unfinished business. The end of the road for unfinished business is illness and disease.

When a passive person relies on another to make choices for him/her, a false sense of power is created in the active party. At the same time, a feeling of lack of ability is confirmed in the passive person. The more that is done for the passive person, the less the person feels the need to do for himself/herself.

Fear and anger generated from feelings of lack of security and self worth grow as dependency grows. Often, the active person in this type of relationship will take on the job of expressing the stored emotional energy of the stifled, passive person. When this happens, the passive person can turn into a victim of his own denied and projected anger. When the active partner stops acting out the passive person's emotions, the passive person is forced to own and express his feelings. When the passive person takes responsibility for personal choices, then there is no longer a useful purpose for the cord. At that point the cord is discarded.

Control Freaks

Control Freaks habitually over-control and manipulate. They need to use someone else's life to exercise their power to make decisions. They feel a lack of power and confidence in their own ability to make choices and decisions for themselves. The creation of a dependent relationship is one way to feel useful, worthy, loved, and appreciated. A person who is too insecure and afraid to use his creative focus on his own life, and thus suffer the cause and effect consequences, will appear fearless when making choices for others.

The role of parenting often creates a victim dynamic between parents and grown children. The children will sometimes acquiesce just to satisfy the "tribal" elders. The children will see the act of giving up their power of choice as an act of love and respect. A true act of love, however, would be to speak his/her truth, thereby rebalancing the energy into a healthy dynamic, rather than nurturing the parental negative energy of control and fear. When the children remain silent, it allows the parents to set control cords. When parents make decisions for the grown children, the children sometimes store internal resentment. A true act of love by the parents would be to release the fear of failure for the children and allow them to exercise their freedom of choice. The parents should encourage the children to learn through experience. Sometimes this path is very difficult for parents, because healthy cords are there for parents to protect their young, inexperienced, dependent children. In healthy relationships, as the children age, the cords are gradually released. However, when the parents are "control freaks," they refuse to release the children to make their own independent decisions and the cords remain intact.

Shadows

When we deny that we are capable of all human attributes and behaviors, we reject the truth of who we are. Remember, we are whole and complete. When we don't want to admit to our full human potential, the good, bad, positive, and negative, we store the rejected parts of ourselves in our shadow.

Even when our judgments and fears are denied, they still exist and hold a negative energy charge. What is inside of us will project outside, regardless of our denial. Consequently, what we fear, judge, and criticize will stand before us. The fact is that the harder that we deny a behavior or feeling, the more forcefully it will emerge in another. The person who receives your shadow projection becomes the object of your judgment and criticism. This person is a scapegoat.

Scapegoats hold the veil of denial for us. They relieve us of the responsibility of acknowledging our own judgment. Scapegoats take on the role of the bad guy, but all they are really doing is magnifying and making visible our fears and judgments. Some cultural and historical scapegoats that have born the brunt of social punishment are women who are labeled witches, prostitutes, gay people, Jewish people, and Jesus Christ.

A Perfect Match

More often than not, two people will attract each other when their shadow issues match. This is how we audition our friends and partners on the energy level. Strong magnetic sparks arise when our shadow energies match. The person who is closest to you is often the person who continually pushes your buttons and stirs up your issues.

This is how it works: You will see yourself as what you think you are. You will see the other as what you deny and reject within yourself. What one person is missing, the other person exhibits. One's strength is the others weakness. This balances the dualistic equation. This system gives a sense of wholeness and completeness to the pair. The problem is that the human potential that you fear or deny, you are rejecting in yourself, therefore you will want to reject it in the other person too.

IDENTITY

I AM	I AM NOT
Feelings and traits that you might choose to own.	Complementary feelings and traits that you disown, deny, and fear, you project onto another.
honest	dishonest
powerful, strong	weak
generous	miserly
sensitive	insensitive
calm	angry
ambitious	not ambitious
interesting	boring
exciting	relaxed
NOT jealous	jealous
responsible	not responsible
financially incapable	financially capable
giver	taker

Shadow issues make us feel very uncomfortable. They cause a lot of friction and fire in relationships. Rather than point a finger at the other person the next time your buttons are pushed, try looking inside. Ask your self, "Can this person be mirroring my own negative energy? Is this trait that bothers me something that I judge and fear within my self? Do I have some unfinished business that I am denying?

If you can learn to recognize your shadow projections, you have an opportunity to deepen the understanding of who you are. When one chooses to examine situations, seeking to identify and own fearful, judgmental, and guilty thoughts, a powerful possibility opens to change those negative thoughts and to express stifled emotions. It follows that the external personal reality must improve, because when magnetic negative energy is released, there is more positive energy flowing that can be used to manifest conscious desires.

Soul maturity requires that we recognize and own our underlying, dualistic feelings of lack. It requires that we acknowledge the good, the bad, and the ugly aspects of our human dualistic selves with love, acceptance, and without judgment. It requires that we face our fears, and demands that we find the courage to do so. When we remember who we really are, that life is just a spirit game, that we are eternal, that the body is only temporary, that we have the power to create a positive reality, that age in the body brings experience and wisdom, and that as magnificent spirit energy we have nothing to lose, then we can learn to laugh at ourselves. When we do that, we take all the power away from the shadow and open the flow of energy to manifest all of our creative power. Jerry Seinfeld made millions of dollars by recreating, with humor, characters that display our shadow issues.

In the movie "*Like Water to Chocolate,*" the youngest daughter feels deprived of marrying the man she loves because her family code requires that the youngest daughter must devote her life to the service of her mother. In the movie we see one of the older daughters attain freedom by taking charge of her life, while the youngest daughter, with great sadness, gives her power to create her life over to her mean, selfish, controlling mother. This main character cannot follow her heart's desire and say, "no" to her mother's control. She becomes resigned to a life of slavery, deprivation, and misery. The mother returns to haunt the daughter even after her death. This appears to be an attempt to rob her daughter of her happiness.

We cringe at the mean over-controlling mother who appears to be the evil enemy, but she is really the scapegoat for the daughter who fears taking responsibility for her own happiness by breaking family law and marrying the man that she loves. The daughter is a victim of her own weakness. Because she is unable to own her power, she projects it onto her mother.

At the end of the movie the daughter realizes that she always had the choice to exercise her right to reject the family agenda and choose happiness. She finds her missing strength. When she overcomes her fears and takes charge of her life, she is set free from what appears to be her mother's curse. This movie is a good example of the consequences of giving one's personal power away to a tribal belief.

Peter Pan, who thinks of himself as a fearless warrior, banishes his fear of growing up to his shadow. The ticking alligator is the scapegoat that reflects the primal fears of temporal life, aging and death. The alligator, a predator that causes Peter to feel unsafe, holds the projection by appearing to be the enemy that is chasing him. Peter's true enemy is his fear of time, experience, growth, and responsibility. The alligator is merely a symbol, an external reflection of Peter's internal fear. It would disappear from Peter's reality if he could conquer his fear. Peter chooses to remain an innocent child, rather than muster up the courage to opt for growth and wisdom within a temporal body. His fear remains locked in his shadow.

I was in a holistic physician's examining room one day when the telephone rang. The doctor answered it. A conversation with another physician ensued regarding a post surgical patient with a severe case of edema. The patient was recovering from surgery to his leg, and the swelling was increasing. The results were baffling the doctors.

The doctor knew that I was a medical intuitive and so I asked him whether he would like some further insight into the case. The doctor gave me the man's first name, and I put in a request to the angels for assistance. I was told that the man was gripped with the fear of aging. He had classic mid-life fears of losing power and virility. I could see that he manifested a problem in his leg because of his fear that he would not be able to stand firmly on his own two legs as he aged. If the man had the cultural background that presented positive benefits connected with aging, which includes the respect and wisdom that accompany maturity, he would not have been suffering from the illness. Instead, he held perceptions of loss of ability and power. He manifested the problem in his right leg, which symbolically represents male energy.

The physician then informed me that even though this man was middle aged, he had just married a very young girl in her twenties. This act clearly exacerbated the problem. While on the surface it might have made this man feel young to be with a youthful partner, deep down he was combining fear of age together with jealousy of her youth and tossing them both into his shadow.

Marrying a significantly younger woman opened a barrage of fearful thoughts for the patient. In addition to his original fears, he had added the fear that as he grew older, he would have a hard time keeping up with his youthful partner. He also added to that the fear that as his wife aged, she might begin to look for a younger man to replace her aged husband. The result was a manifestation of physical symptoms in his body.

While walking arm in arm with youth might have seemed to calm this man's fears at the time of his marriage, it went on to multiply them and bring them to fruition. Getting to know his shadow motivations prior to choosing a wife might have averted the manifestation of physical problems. It was clear that this man had some serious work to do to identify, process, and resolve his fears, before he would be able to permanently heal and stand on healthy legs again.

Much of the dust that I see in the energy field results from shadow issues that are unconsciously stored away. Shadow energies are a large part of the reason that the victim perspective is so prevalent. When we are unaware of the negative emotional energy that we build and hold on to, it has great power to insidiously produce an unwanted and seemingly uncontrollable personal reality. Shadow energies motivate our internal saboteur.

By moving shadow issues into the foreground and dealing with them, we remove their ominous power to insidiously control circumstances that appear to victimize us. It takes a great deal of courage to deal with shadow issues. It is because of our fear of admitting our judgments and weaknesses that banishes them to the shadow in the first place. Looking at the shadow is the equivalent of opening Pandora's box.

Finding the Center of Duality

Throughout this book, I talk about learning to own your own energy. Let me take a moment to be clear about what I mean when I use these words. Co-dependent behavior exhibits the expression of one side of a dualistic concept, and it rejects the potential for the other half. For example, a passive person rejects his aggressive traits. Another example would be when a responsible person pairs up with candidate to hold his irresponsible shadow. In each of these examples, one half of the pair is standing on the extreme right or left side of the duality line. This person refuses to see and act according to the opposite polarity within himself and must pull in another person to exhibit these complementary traits in order to complete the whole concept.

When a person chooses to see all of his own human potential, without rejection or judgment, and he knows that he has the ability to choose to use whatever traits he feels are appropriate at each particular moment in time, he is standing in the center of the duality line. In the center there is conscious awareness of possible access to any place on the conceptual duality line. When a person finds his center, he understands that somewhere inside of him is the same potential for a thief and a murderer to exist, as there is for a hero to exist. In the center, one understands that on the earth plane, in order to have wealth, there must also be poverty. He knows that in order to have an aging population, we must have a youthful population. Neither extreme can exist without its polar opposite. The person knows that throughout his or her soul history he or she will exhibit many extreme behaviors. Even though the individual path may take us to the far ends of both roads, we must eventually ride the elevator up through the center of duality to find our way home. The center is a place where there is no judgment. The center is the place where we simply know "I am that I am." It is where we find compassion and gratitude.

Therefore, when I talk about holding your own energy, I am talking about owning the good, bad, and ugly possibilities of all human behavior. I am talking about recognizing and accepting that to be human means to experience all possible qualities and behaviors. Being human affords an opportunity to understand the value of each experience based on the knowledge gained. All experiences add to the bank of knowledge that we rely on to exercise our free will power of choice.

The Positive Purpose of Negative Emotions

A good rule of thumb is to face, embrace, and release all emotions. All emotions need to be acknowledged rather than judged, denied, and banished. The universe doesn't waste energy. No matter what form it takes, energy always offers an opportunity for you to come to know your own power and truth. Every emotion can be used in a positive or negative way. You must own all of your energy. When you are able to embrace it and listen to it, you will learn about your individual ego personality. After all, isn't that why we are here?

Anger and jealousy are red flags that have a purpose. Jealousy can identify particular specific thoughts of lack and limitation. Jealousy can be a very positive force that notifies us of our desires and presents opportunities to crystallize future goals. Many people have a very difficult time knowing what they want. To create something in life, one must first know what he or she wants and then have an intention to have it. Observing in another what you think you want for yourself, presents you with a menu of new possibilities. Developing the ability to acknowledge and use jealousy in a positive way will neutralize and release the negative energy of the emotion. If, on the other hand, jealousy is allowed to fester, it can grow and become a monster that interferes with relationships and causes the manufacture of more negative energy in the field. Jealousy can lead to anger and judgment. The ego-self can have a picnic with jealousy.

Anger can be a very positive force if you seek its message. Anger can light up shadow issues. In this way it can serve as an alarm that signals you to pay attention to your feelings and get to work on yourself, rather than on other people. Anger can also alert you to the fact that someone is encroaching on your boundaries. It can reveal to you that you must get in touch with your power. If someone is about to grab your power by setting a cord, remaining silent is a good way to help assist him or her. The result will be a victim feeling within you. In contrast, finding and using your voice to express your boundaries will shift your own power back into your own court, thus the cord will not be accepted. Hearing your own voice can lead to a massive dose of self-validation. Therefore, anger can be a catalyst to initiate action toward positive change.

Giving Power to Fear

Fear is the perception of lack. You can only be held hostage to fear when you are blocked from knowing that your true creative power lies within you. This is the veil of the earth plane. This perception of lack of power brings on a state of vulnerability. That which you perceive that you do not have, but desperately want, can be sold to you for the price of your soul. When you feel as if you are sacrificing your integrity, look for the fear and find its counterpart truth on the "I AM" list. Only the truth can set you free.

If you banish your fear to your shadow, it will become very difficult to find your integrity again. You will magnetize many new tests of conflict between your heart and your fears of lack. This is a very popular earth plane lesson.

One common scenario where fear controls one's life is with women who desperately want to leave stale unsatisfying relationships, but are afraid to stand on their own financial legs. They doubt their ability to manifest because they have not previously taken charge and exercised their power to create financial safety and security.

When a female parental model is uninvolved in the family finances, the adult female offspring can imprint a feeling of incompetence in the financial arena. On the other hand, a woman who chooses to work through her fears and negative perceptions can benefit from the opportunity to grow by developing these innate abilities.

Chapter 5

Chakras and Quadrants

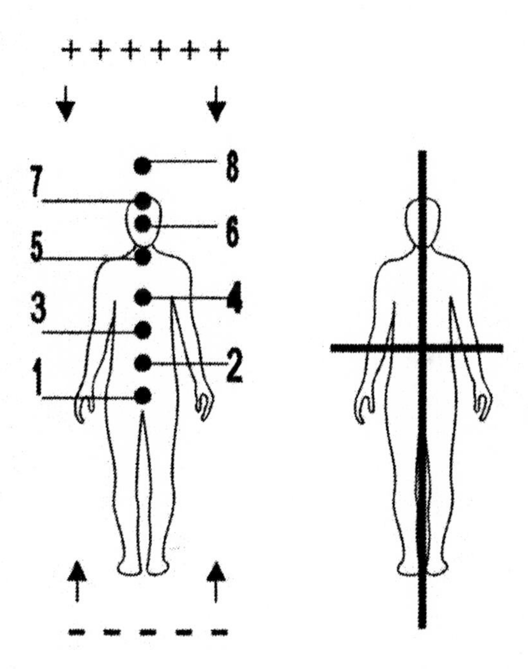

Chakra is the name given to each energy center that processes the energy of human experience. There are eight known charkas in the energy field. They are located on the vertical axis of the body, beginning at the groin and running up to and above the top of the head. The opening of each doorway presents us with the ongoing choice of whether to leave home, opting for a perception of separation, which holds a negative energetic charge, or whether to return home by remembering our wholeness, which holds a positive energetic charge. We anchor feelings of separation, lack, and limitation in our first through third charkas.

Chakra 1

The Illusion Begins

Humpty Dumpty had a great fall.

Choice: unity or separation

The first chakra anchors us to the earth plane. Negative energy enters the body through this gateway. This chakra assists in the building of our ego personality by fostering the illusion of separation. Feeling separate leads to feelings of lack of power, which initiates fear. It is the job of the ego-self to harbor and emit fear. The fear of death and the instinct to survive are first chakra programs that come with our limited human form.

The first chakra is a meat grinder. It processes energy that tells us that we are many separate people rather than one whole Spirit-being. In this chakra, negative energy initiates doubts about our safety and security in relation to the external world. Here, negative energy serves to negate the truth of our unified, internal spiritual connection. It leads us to believe that there is safety and power in numbers. We learn to believe that our power to survive lies in our affiliations with other individuals and groups, such as our family, tribe, race or country.

This chakra is where we imprint our tribal group agendas and inherited karma. The consciousness of the culture is absorbed here. This is where cellular ancestral thoughts, such as beliefs about life, disease, scarcity, aging, and death are recycled and reinforced.

SEPARATION (FEAR) = LACK OF POWER

Symptoms, Issues, and Lessons

Victim consciousness (lack of creative power) is a function of the first chakra. A person holding on to victim consciousness creates blocks on the energy field and manifests these blocks as physical problems in the lower torso, hands, wrists, and legs. Carpal tunnel syndrome is an indication of blame that arises out of a victim perspective. Being accident-prone is the most obvious symbol of victim consciousness.

Taking responsibility for one's own choice of thoughts, beliefs, and actions, without assigning blame, is the path to overcoming the effects of victim energy. Releasing the negative energy of fear and affirming one's connection to the whole Spirit-Self and its unlimited internal power to create abundance is the way to overcome the challenges of the first chakra. When we triumph over this challenge, we become independent, courageous, and strong human beings.

Chakra 2

Duality: You and Me

Humpty Dumpty feels separated.
He is frightened and confused.
He wonders, "Do I or don't I exist?
Who or what am I now?"

Choice: perception of lack or abundance (Empty or Full)

The duality of opposites and the number two are the underlying themes of the second chakra. The individual soul must experience both sides of many dualistic emotional equations (the Tree of Good and Evil), spanning the entire range of human emotions, to complete its human journey.

The second chakra processes information that fosters the illusion that you and I are two separate individuals and form a relationship with one another. Comparing one person with the other initiates perceptions of lack. Feelings such as lack power, lack of control, lack of safety, lack of support, lack of money, lack of material possessions, and lack of opportunity are produced. Perceptions of lack invoke deep-seated feelings of need, judgment, enemy conflict, doubt, insecurity, anger, frustration, resignation, blame, resentment, and hate. These negative emotions can become embedded in this area of the energy field.

Symptoms, Issues, and Lessons

The second chakra is the busiest area for me to read while serving as a medical intuitive. More can be learned about the human condition in this particular section of the energy field than in any other. Rarely do I see an energy field that does not contain some dust in this vicinity. Physical problems that arise out of blocks in the second chakra are not limited to manifest only in this section of the body. Negative energy registered here can and does affect the entire body.

We use the second chakra to originate and implement our ideas about what we want to do with our lives. This is the center of our creative God-Self power. When we are not using our creative abilities, or we are not aware of how to use them in a positive way, negative creations arise in many forms, including the appearance of internal lumps and bumps. Many physical problems that arise in this area of the body serve as distractions from having to face fears and take positive action towards creating the goals and challenges necessary for producing personal health and happiness. Illness can be a scapegoat for the creatively inept, fearful or even lazy person.

Peter Pan Syndrome, the fear of growing up and taking responsibility for one's own happiness, shows itself in the area of the second chakra. People with this syndrome can spend most of their lives stuck in unsatisfying work and relationships while their lives pass them by merely because they either can NOT muster up the courage to face their fears, or they think that there aren't any other options, or they are just too lazy to seek out and create alternative solutions that will be meaningful and fulfilling. Hidden repressed fears that inhibit positive action can cause extensive weight gain and weight loss.

The second chakra is the place where we process emotions that deal with relationships. Power plays and security issues fester in this section of the energy field. Feelings of lack of support can register as low back and hip problems. Unprocessed emotions such as anger, resentment, and blame can lodge in any of the organs in this area below the waist as well as in the hands and wrists. They can stop up the bowel causing constipation. Excessive and constant fear might cause diarrhea or other stomach problems. Negative feelings about masculine and feminine energy can manifest illness in and around the sexual organs.

When we remember our true connection to the other, "I am that I am," we open the positive flow of energy through this doorway. A positive flow harnesses our unlimited creative abilities. We use this energy to take action to create satisfying ways to enjoy our lives. When this chakra is processing positive energy, we see abundance. With that vision we create feelings of safety, security, beauty, friendship, gratitude, and reverence.

Chakra 3

Identity, Self Worth, and Self Love

> Humpty realizes that only his shell is broken. He discovers that his inner self is whole. He feels okay about himself.

Choice: self approval or self judgment

This chakra holds the dualistic perceptions and feelings about the self. Who am I? What am I doing here? Am I valuable? When we do not have a rich positive flow of energy through the third chakra, we crimp the positive energy flow through the other chakras. A healthy positive identity seems to push open the doors both above and below it. The third chakra appears to be the master switch to the whole lighting system. When it is blocked with negative energy, the whole place is dark.

The third chakra processes the following negative thoughts and feelings:

I am small.
I am nothing
I am not able.
I am not worthy.
I do not have any power.
I am not good enough.
I am not smart enough.
I need you to validate me.

Symptoms, Issues, and Lessons

Feelings of depression, self-loathing, and self-pity arise from this energy center. When there is negative energy in the third chakra, there is difficulty in getting in touch with one's value and potential. Feeling unable to acquire a satisfying partner, interesting career, money, control of addictions, and freedom from abusive behavior all stem from a lack of confidence in one's abilities and feelings of unworthiness. Third chakra issues of self-judgment and guilt can open the doorway to hell. Acne and skin problems can result from feeling ugly. Auto-immune diseases can have their root in the negative energy running through the third chakra.

It Begins in Childhood

I cannot even begin to count the many people that have come to me in whom I have seen what looks like a tear the size of a bowling ball in the solar plexus area of the energy field. These deep-seated wounds are due to many reasons, but by far the most common causes originate during early childhood. When a parent is abusive, either physically or verbally, the child registers dust in the energy field due to feelings of misconduct and guilt. The same is true when an adult continually condemns and criticizes a child. When a family religion forces children to repeat the words, "I am not worthy," the children become programmed for the remainder of their lives to reject their true God-Self roots and heritage of abundance. This is also true when children are ignored or silenced because they receive the message that they are not worthy of attention. Poverty and financial problems that occur later in life are often the result of these messages.

The positive flow of energy through this center affirms:

Positive self worth
Self-love – " I count too."
I am worthy of love.
I am worthy to receive gifts.
I deserve
I respect myself.
I honor myself.

The ability to project a positive reality requires the ability to see your-self in a positive light.

Chakra 4

Seat of the Emotions

Humpty is much happier now that he has discarded his shell. He feels grateful for his journey, including the fall. This birthing process, has taught him that his strength lies in his essence, not in his exterior shell. Now he doesn't have to be afraid anymore. He knows that his essence cannot be destroyed. He no longer has a reason to feel guilty or blame himself for the fall. He feels reconnected to all there is.

Choice: unconditional love and compassion or pain

Feelings of love and gratitude connect us back to our truth. This is not to be mixed up with feelings of wanting and needing to be loved, which is the expression and perception of lack of love. This produces feelings of more lack, according to the Law of Multiplication. Let me be clear. Many people will say, “I love you,” but what they are really saying is, “I need your attention and validation.” This is not love, but lack, and is the root cause of dissatisfaction with life and relationships. When we are motivated from feelings of lack, we feel a need to fill the inner emptiness and seek to obtain the fullness from an external other. This solution is like trying to fill a bucket that has a hole in the bottom. This approach to relationships results in an endless pattern of continuous needing, taking, wanting, and seeking.

When I use the word love, I mean a feeling of caring and appreciation that does not require anything in return. We can love people, places, activities, and things. When we reconnect with our true heart’s desires, we find that we are motivated out of joy. The fullness that we seek from others can only come from reconnecting with our own internal Spirit-Self, because the external other can only serve to mirror our own projection of the feelings that we hold about ourselves. This reconnection brings on feelings of fullness, joy, and gratitude for life. When this occurs, we attract another toward us who has the ability to mirror these positive feelings back to us.

The fourth chakra is the seat of our emotions. Emotions propel mental thoughts and visions into physical manifestations. When strong emotions are connected to a thought, it manifests more quickly and fully in our physical reality.

When we are unwilling to feel pain, we unknowingly block the energy flow in our fourth chakra. Sometimes we do this because tribal agendas teach us that it is not acceptable to feel or express emotions such as grief, sadness, and anger. This is very harmful behavior. When we store painful emotions, we empower them to attract more situations that ignite additional pain within us. The heart chakra must remain open for it to process feelings and manifest our heart's desires.

Symptoms, Issues, and Lessons

Negative energy clouds form in the heart and lung area due to grief, disappointment, betrayal, feeling hurt, and feeling unloved. When we have learned not to trust, we close down our heart charkas. Clouds that form in this area can cause heart problems, breathing problems, and digestive problems. When an emotion gets stuck, it blocks the resolution of subsequent emotions, as well as the digestion of food. I have seen long term, unresolved grief create hiatal hernia and other severe problems with digestion. When the pain of loss is stored, it will attract more negative experience to the person, such as more disappointment, hurt, rejection, abandonment, etc. Holding on to negative emotions is a toxic way to live life. It disconnects the person from consciously processing new experiences and feelings. Often, people will come to me and exclaim, "After the death of so and so," or "After my break up with so and so, my life seemed to go down hill." That is when I explain to them that we need to learn to face, embrace, and release our painful emotions in order to clear the energy field of debris that blocks the natural positive flow of energy and holds us to the past. Both positive and negative emotions need to be deeply felt and then released, allowing the person to live a full and satisfying life in each moment, as it occurs. One way to release our painful feelings is to express them. In this light, crying and anger serve a healing purpose.

Judgments held as third chakra blocks give birth to fourth chakra issues that deal with lack of forgiveness. Lack of forgiveness holds us to anger, resentment, and blame. These third and fourth chakra blocks cause additional blocks to form in the fifth chakra, the home of vocal expression.

Chakra 5

Seat of Expression, Release, Change, and Choice

> Humpty can now let go of the yearning to be whole again because he knows that he is and always was whole. He says, "I am who I am right now." He releases the need to retrieve his shell. He gifts it to the earth, blesses it, and moves on with gratitude.

Choice: to hold on to the ego-self or let it go

The fifth chakra is the chakra of the voice, the will, release, change, and choice. The act of using ones voice is an act of release and empowerment.

Symptoms, Issues, and Lessons

The fifth chakra houses the energy of the will. A decision to change must come from the will. Many internal battles between the heart and the mind are begun in the area of the fourth and fifth chakra when fear faces off with desire. The thyroid gland can suffer the effects of the battle together with the heart, the lung, and the thymus gland. Tension in the neck and shoulders also results from the stress produced.

Resistance to the release of negative and limiting behavior patterns, beliefs, emotions, and thoughts results in the formation of energy blocks in the fifth chakra. Restrictions of personal expression due to laziness, resignation, fear, shame, or even grief will cause problems with the teeth, gums, jaw, throat, thyroid, esophagus, and vocal cords. Shortness of breath and hiatal hernia can also develop. The expression, *lump in your throat,* implies that fear can lodge and block expression. This is exactly what happens on the energy field. Children that are taught not to question or confront adults form massive blocks in their fifth chakras.

Chakra 6

Insight

Humpty Dumpty finds a whole in the wall and sees through to the other side. He sees things differently now. Humpty realizes that his break was actually a breakthrough to a whole new level of perception.

Choice: to remove the veil and see truth beyond illusion.

The sixth chakra is the location of the third eye. It is our connection to the inner world of spirit. The sixth chakra provides the ability to perceive the larger truth beyond the illusion that is seen by the outer eyes. This is where we have the ability to both create and receive visions. Development of inner sight is a doorway to the spiritual guidance that will lead a person back home to an enlightened perspective.

Symptoms, Issues, and Lessons

Problems with the eyes and ears occur when we do not want to see and hear the truth. These symbols can serve as wake up calls that signal us to look for denial within. Headaches and ear problems can also result from loud expressions of anger and abuse in the home.

Chakra 7

Returning Home

> Humpty forgets that he is an egg. He only knows that he exists. He feels peaceful and complete.

Choice: to accept peace and harmony or NOT

The seventh chakra is the crown chakra, the doorway that receives positive energy from the spiritual dimension. Rejection of one's spiritual guidance to perceive truth can cause restrictions in this energy flow.

Symptoms, Issues, and Lessons

Stress, worry, inner conflict, and excess sensual stimulation can cause this chakra to become blocked. Headaches are often created out of a desire to manifest an escape from reality. When a person feels trapped, he/she will create a migraine headache to shut down the perceptual mechanisms. Meditation, visualization, hands on healing, positive affirmations, relaxation, and intention to release worry can help to open this chakra. An intentional focus on opening up the energy flow through this chakra can bring feelings of peace, harmony, and wholeness.

Chakra 8

Seeing the Big Picture

Humpty sees himself as part of a larger whole. He begins to see and know his importance as a symbolic mythical figure. Humpty learns the whole truth and laughs. What a yoke!

Choice: To Participate on the Earth Plane

The eighth chakra holds the history and goals that underlie temporal illusion. It contains all of the information that connects people places, things, and events past, present, and future. It holds the blueprints for the lessons of our individual lives as well as for the larger story for the ages. We cannot see the big pictures from our individual points of view. Much of what we see looks disconnected. In actuality, each individual is a microcosm as well as an indispensable part of an evolutionary macrocosm.

If we could see into the information held in the eighth chakra, we would each know how valuable every person is to the whole manifestation of human history. The larger meaning and purpose of our lives is hidden in the higher vibrations. If we work hard and persist on the spiritual path to enlightenment, we can catch a glimpse of the threads to these incredibly detailed webs. Meditation is the express train to this destination.

Level 9

Angels, Music, and Creative Vibrations

I do not know this to be factual, however, I can recall a meditation once when a guide took me through many dimensions of consciousness. I recall experiencing the most beautiful musical vibrations in what I believed at the time to be a ninth level of vibration. This is still my chosen belief. I suggest that you do your own research.

The following chart indicates which chakras are affected on the "I Am Not" list

The "I Am NOT" List

The Veil of Denial of Internal Creative Power

The "Not' list delineates the energy that is carried when one identifies with the separate ego-self and perceives oneself to be lacking. This is the list of issues that emerge within the human condition. Negative energy is created with every denial of the truth of the existence of internal creative power and wholeness. Each "NOT" contains a negative electrical charge.

FEELING……………..……..PERCEPTION……..CHAKRA

- I feel and/ or know that
something is missing in my life………….. NOT whole …..1,2

- I feel powerless to change my
external circumstances..……..……………….NOT powerful …..1,2

- I am focused on getting
and achieving what I do not have…………NOT having = lack ……..2

- I am focused on satisfying
the needs that I perceive I have…………….NOT having =lack ……..2

- I fear the loss of what I have……..NOT safe & secure ……..2

- I fear being controlled
by another…………………..…..…NOT in control ……..2

- I fear not having money
and security………….…..……….. NOT safe & secure ……..2

FEELING......................**PERCEPTION**.......**CHAKRA**

- I fear being alone, unloved, and unappreciated.....NOT loved, valued and .... supported ... 1,2,3
- I don't have any reason to feel valuable. ....NOT worthy 3
- I must prove my worth to others............ ......NOT owning worth, esteem 3
- I am not good enough.................NOT good enough 2,3
- I feel and create judgment, guilt, and blame..........NOT good enough 2,3
- I fear being judged by others......NOT self approving 3,4

When we decide to go on vacation from the unified truth of who we are, we pack a suitcase full of the preceding human issues.

All Four Quadrants Must Be In Balance

When I do an energy field scan, I can see the energy field on my inner screen. The energy flows through four quadrants. Each quadrant represents two overlapping dualistic aspects of the human journey. The energy flowing through all four quadrants must be in balance for a person to manifest health and happiness.

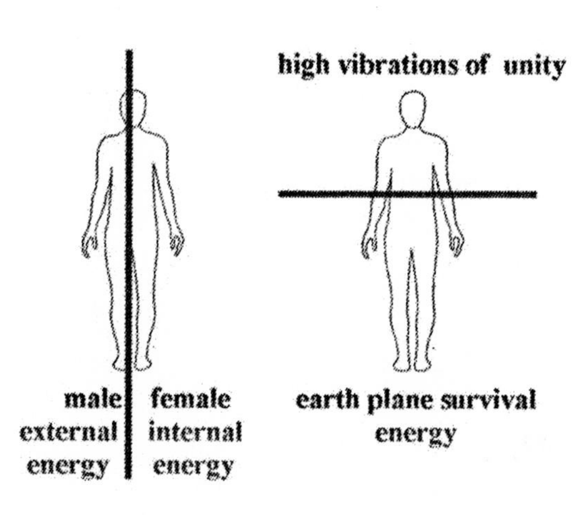

The right and left sides of the energy field represent the male and female aspects of each person. The upper and lower quadrants represent the higher and lower frequencies of the energy of unity and separation. An open flow to all four quadrants creates physical, mental, and emotional health.

The four quadrants are situated in the body's energy field in the following way: The body's field is divided in half vertically with the left side controlled by the right brain. And the right side controlled by the left brain. The right brain is our creative brain. It processes the internal, female energy within every individual. The female energy is creative, emotional, and nurturing. It houses the imagination and the intuitive receptors. The left brain controls patriarchal, male energy. It processes logical, linear, rational thought. It also nourishes the separate ego-self. The male, patriarchal energy is active energy and relates to external form and the survival of the body.

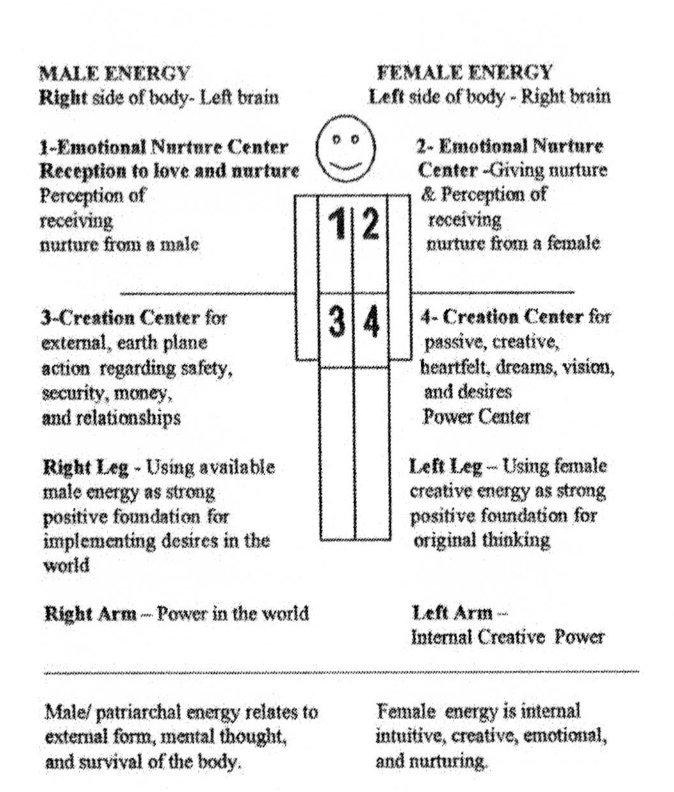
MALE ENERGY
Right side of body- Left brain
FEMALE ENERGY
Left side of body - Right brain
1-Emotional Nurture Center
Reception to love and nurture
Perception of
receiving
nurture from a male
2- Emotional Nurture
Center -Giving nurture
& Perception of
receiving
nurture from a female
1
2
3
4
3-Creation Center for
external, earth plane
action regarding safety,
security, money,
and relationships
4- Creation Center for
passive, creative,
heartfelt, dreams, vision,
and desires
Power Center
Right Leg - Using available
male energy as strong
positive foundation for
implementing desires in the
world
Left Leg – Using female
creative energy as strong
positive foundation for
original thinking
Right Arm – Power in the world
Left Arm –
Internal Creative Power
Male/ patriarchal energy relates to
external form, mental thought,
and survival of the body.
Female energy is internal
intuitive, creative, emotional,
and nurturing.

#1 - THE UPPER RIGHT QUADRANT processes feelings, perceptions, and beliefs about male examples, attitudes, and behaviors. The following energy is processed in the upper right quadrant:

- Father as model / imprinting and feelings about:
  Father's nurturing patterns
  Father's communication patterns
  Father's emotional patterns
- Ability to receive nurturing
- Balance of mental and emotional energy (feeling or blocking the emotions)
- Perception of personal importance to parents, family world, and self
- Past and present judgment of male
- Past and present regrets of being male
- Past and present fears of males
- Disappointment from males
- Attitudes about being male and strength of male energy

#3 – THE LOWER RIGHT QUADRANT processes feelings, perceptions, and beliefs about male energy that deals with earthly matters. The following energy is processed in the lower right quadrant:

- Action taken to create external reality
- Creating safety, security, worldly desires, and survival needs
- Perception of male support from child and adult perspectives
- Past and present blame of male
- Perception of support from worldly institutions, ie. corporations
- Satisfaction in career
- Accepting male cultural norms as personal agenda

RIGHT LEG – Indicates the ability to stand on patriarchal foundation and function well in the world.

#2 - THE UPPER LEFT QUADRANT processes feelings, perceptions, and beliefs about female nurturing, female attitudes, and female models. The following energy is processed in the upper left quadrant:

- Mother as model / imprinting, feelings and perception about:
  mother's nurturing patterns
  mother's emotional patterns
  mother's communication patterns
- Ability to nurture and be nurtured
- Past and present judgment towards women
- Past and present regrets regarding being female
- Past and present fears regarding women
- Attitudes and beliefs about being female
- Perception of female power and worth

#4 – THE LOWER LEFT QUADRANT processes feelings, perceptions, and beliefs about female creative power. The following energy is processed in the lower left quadrant:

- Perception of abilities
- Perception of potential
- Perception of possibilities
- Perception of limitations
- Creating an individual agenda including fulfilling goals and career
- Appreciating and/or participating in the arts
- Perception of having female support
- Past and present blame for women

LEFT LEG – Indicates the ability to stand on the female energetic foundation and make positive use of personal, creative, female energy.

THE UPPER QUADRANTS

The upper quadrants of the energy field, #1 and #2, are the nurture centers. The left #2 quadrant processes feelings of being loved and nurtured. It also processes the feelings of giving out nurturing. When the inner child perceives a lack of nurturing from the mother figure, this perception will show up as a block in the upper left quadrant. When the individual perceives a lack of nurturing from the father, or another significant male figure, a block will show up on the upper right quadrant.

Balancing Give and Take

The right side of the energy field processes thought energy and the lefts side processes feelings. When a person leans too heavily on thinking and rejects processing emotions, the imbalance shows up as a block on the right upper quadrant in the heart-lung area. This energy dynamic of imbalance underlies heart disease.

Many women adopt the dysfunctional pattern of giving too much nurturing. When there is an imbalance of giving and receiving, the individual unconsciously creates and stores anger and resentment. This kind of imbalance is detrimental to one's health. The result is the equivalent of adding a resentment marble to one side of a scale of justice each time an energy imbalance is felt. Eventually, the scale must tip over causing enough chaos to change the situation. Negative energy builds until it explodes into manifestations of illness and projected trauma, signaling the person to seek a way to cure the imbalance. There must be an equitable exchange of give and take energy in relationships for health to flourish.

The spirit doesn't care what kind of behavioral characteristics are sanctioned by the tribe as good or bad. It doesn't care what the individual thinks it should do to be a lovable person. The spirit knows that it is worthy and perfect. The spirit is the part of us that wants to be happy and grateful for life. We must allow our spirit to enjoy life. When we fill our lives with "shoulds," responsibilities, caring for others and too much work, our spirit rebels in an effort to get us to create energetic equilibrium by attracting some circumstance that will call for the person to stop giving and start receiving.

Illness is sometimes created as a way to force us to be still and receive from others. Women who are always giving and not receiving manifest imbalance in the form of heart, lung, and breast problems. Women who are feeling an underlying lack of nurturing are in epidemic proportions, thus the amount of women with breast cancer continues to grow. If a person recovers from one of these illnesses and resumes the old patterns, he or she will begin to repeat the loop, whereby the same traumatic results will occur again, perhaps with different circumstances and a whole new set of people. When an energy imbalance remains, an unwanted reality will also remain.

Self Love

Not only must active nurturers allow themselves to receive from others, it is absolutely necessary for each person to be self-loving. Many tribal agendas teach that to be selfless is an admirable goal. Contrary to this dogma, the energy field requires that the individual recognize the original truth that I am you and you are me. I must recognize and honor myself, as well as the other person. When we love and respect ourselves, the outside world reflects our feelings. What a happy world this would be if we could all aspire to this goal.

The third chakra of self-love and self-worth sits at the intersection of the four quadrants. How we see and feel about ourselves is the key to our spiritual journey. When we achieve the state of knowing the "I am that I am," we think and act with the ultimate respect and love for ourselves as well as others. With this knowledge we have the key to open the door to heaven on earth.

THE LOWER QUADRANTS

The lower quadrants, #3 and #4, are the creative energy centers. The lower left quadrant #4 processes the energy of hopes, dreams and visions, the products of the imagination. This is the power center. The imagination is the vehicle for the initiation of power. After all, everything starts with an idea.

We are naturally endowed with an abundance of creative potential, yet both men and women have problems activating the power within their lower left quadrant. The power of the imagination is greatly underestimated in our society. All the geniuses in history have used this positive energy. However, with the elimination of the arts in the schools, and an emphasis put on left-brain scientific and intellectual capabilities, many people are ignorant when it comes to knowing how to use their creative abilities. In addition, when there is a male or female parental model whose positive energy flow is blocked to this quadrant, the child has a difficult time learning how to use this energy. This is the equivalent of having a computer, but not knowing how to use the equipment. When this quadrant is blocked, boredom, despair, a sense of entrapment, and loneliness can turn into illness.

Men and women who live their lives by accepting that the external reality is rigidly set, and that they must find a way to fit into it, rather than create it, do great damage to their bodies. When the lower left creative quadrant is not used, various health problems ensue that require removal of organs. Many women who don't use their creative powers have had to have surgery for the removal of fibroid tumors, cysts, ovaries, and the uterus.

I recently did a health scan on a woman with a blocked lower left quadrant. She told me that she had just had a medical exam and that her doctor could not find her left ovary. She had never had it removed and could not understand how this could be possible. I told her that the message that the universe was giving to her was to use it or lose it.

Whatever is created on the lower left side, #4, with the female passive energy is implemented in the world with the male active energy of the lower right quadrant, #3. Quadrant #3 processes the energy that we use to create safety, security, money, and career. The right side, #3, will indicate how we are functioning in the outside world. For example, we create the idea for a business from the lower left quadrant. We implement that idea with the energy of the lower right quadrant.

Someone might have a clear and open energy path on the right side, be doing very well in life and still be manifesting serious illness because he or she is not creating a personal agenda from the energy bank in the lower left quadrant. Cooking, sewing, crafts, music, poetry, meditation, Reiki, and creative visualization are some ways to activate and open up stagnant energy in the lower left quadrant.

Our Patriarchal Society

The individual that is brought up in a particular culture reflects the energy of that culture. Our society is predominantly a patriarchal society. The result is a lack of respect for and validation of the female energy, both in the female individual as well as the female aspects within each male. Consequently, we live in a culture that idolizes rationalization and science, but rejects the value of the creative arts, intuition, and emotion. Attention to the arts has become practically non-existent in our schools. Men are taught to think and not to feel. Nurturing, creative males are mocked. Women who are working full time jobs and taking care of the house and the family often neglect their own well-being by not taking any time to nurture themselves. Sexual abuse of children is prevalent and pervasive in our society. These are all the results of our rejection and lack of respect for our internal female aspects.

Cultural agenda has a large effect on which blocks manifest on the personal energy field. Both men and women have male and female energy. Unfortunately, our society encourages males to use and express only male energy. When this occurs, they reject the female energy and hide it in their shadow. Until the last twenty years, women were required to stay in the kitchen and be the caretakers. They were required to hold their female energy and store their male energy in their shadow. This has been the pattern for the marriage archetype, where each sex draws in the opposite sex to hold its shadow energy so that the relationship can achieve balance. Consequently, co-dependency still remains a rampant and socially acceptable pattern. Women were, and in many instances still are, expected to give the power of decision and choice over to the male patriarch. American women only began to find their voice in the 1960's. They still have a long way to go to break the old dysfunctional patterns. Many men are still refusing to feel and process their own emotions, and they continue to close down their ears to the voices of women. Male children learn from their fathers to banish their feelings to their shadow. As a result, young boys are finding themselves bringing their anger and resentment to school with them as guns and other explosives. The violent, heinous acts of young males are a problem resulting from the unnatural repression of emotions that need to find expression.

The U.S. Congress accurately reflects the proportion of power that the patriarchal society assigns to female energy. I am not saying that men take power from women. I am saying that women give it away, and men accept the dominance and don't want to give the power back. Today's women have inherited the task of retrieving the energy which generations of grandmothers have divested themselves of. It is time for the pendulum to swing back toward the center point. The onset of the twenty-first century is a turning point. The roles of men and women are being redefined according to a more balanced paradigm.

When I scan an energy field, it is not unusual for me to find the upper right quadrant blocked in males and the lower left quadrant blocked in both males and females. This is the result of a patriarchal bias to our culture. Many health problems that are common in our society are due to cultural, energetic, gender imbalances. When men refuse to open their hearts, feel, and process emotions, they close down the flow to the fourth chakra area, producing physical problems in the heart and lung area. Anger and sorrow must be processed, no matter what gender you are. Men and women who have a habit of holding on to grief will sometimes manifest this emotion in the form of a hiatal hernia in the area of their fourth and fifth chakra.

Sometimes the imbalance flips. When a woman in a relationship is the controlling, dominant voice, she pushes the relationship out of balance. When the male does not hold his own energy and right of personal choice, he opens himself up to develop problems in his prostate, gums and teeth, which are centers of power and voice.

Both men and women generally have a problem keeping their fifth chakra clear and open. This is the area of speaking up and expressing feelings. While they allow themselves to feel, they stop short of completing the process with expression. Many young girls are taught that silence is a lady- like virtue. Many children are taught that it is impolite to question and confront. This pattern of silencing expression can cause tremendous damage to the body in the throat, heart, and lung area, and to the quality of life years after emotions are withheld.

I find that men are more congruent in the career areas that they choose than women. Men tend to allow themselves to be drawn to work that harmonizes with their patriarchal energy, while women who give considerable thought to choosing and preparing for a career, sometimes move toward the careers that offer more money. The fact is that our culture pays more for left-brain, patriarchal work such as accounting, corporate careers, and law than it does for the right brain, feminine careers, such as nursing. Because of this, some women who choose to be financially responsible ignore their talents and interests, effectively selling their hearts and souls for security. This kind of conflict between mind and heart creates turmoil in the energy field. Whenever we sell out to our fears, we create lots of resentments and negative energy that resides in the second and third chakra.

Chronic fatigue and fibromyalgia are diseases found more often in women. My readings indicate that an overwhelming feeling of resignation and a need to escape brings on these diseases. Both of these diseases arise out of deep internal feelings of inner conflict. Quite often I see them in women who are working in patriarchal jobs, but are not personally fulfilled by their work. These women feel paralyzed to make the necessary changes in their life, so instead they create diseases that render them helpless to continue to work in a field that they cannot tolerate. When these diseases are active, I find that most of the left side of the entire energy field is blocked, including the arms and legs. In addition, the right lower quadrant and leg are blocked, which indicates that the person is not functioning happily in the work environment. Access to female energy is unavailable because the person is unaware of the possibility of creating a positive solution. A negative attitude shuts the body down so that the person is forced to leave the everyday life pattern that she is leading, but can't bear. The disease offers a reason to hide away for a while and hibernate. Eventually, the woman will get bored and frustrated. At that point she will begin to change her will and start to think about living a fulfilling life. However, when the energy field and the body are shut down for long periods of time, it is very difficult to clear the blocks and open up to a natural healthy energetic flow again.

Part II

Putting It All Together

Chapter 6

Readings

How You Create Your Future

The future is made up of an abundance of possibilities. When I look into the energy of an individual's future, I see lines of possibility and probability. One level of our energy holds blueprints of our thoughts and belief systems, while another level holds our sacred contracts for our chosen lessons.

Within this book I have attempted to capture the universal lessons that we all choose to learn. The ways in which we choose to learn them are all individual soul creations. Experiences and feelings are very personal. I have to this day never met anyone who has completed a difficult lesson, (having absorbed the nectar from the fruit), who would choose to turn back the clock and undo his/her personal experience, despite all the pain and difficulty suffered. Somewhere within us all is the unspoken understanding that the dualities of life hold rich and rewarding experiences. When the light finally dawns and we look back, we cherish every moment of darkness. We all seem to look back with a chuckle. Even though we may have screamed and moaned all the way through the journey, when we achieve our growth, the process appears to have been worthwhile.

While we are in the midst of the darkness, however, life can be a frustrating, ever so slow and grueling climb up the proverbial mountain. We all tend to repeat our self-destructive energetic creations over and over and over again. As long as we continue to create and hold on to negative energy, the external manifestation will leave us feeling powerless. As long as we continue to seek our power externally, we will continue to give our power away to illusionary realities. As long as we put the cart before the horse by believing that the external world is fortuitous, rather than understanding that we have the thoughts and emotions that create the manifestations of physical form, we will be like rats chasing our tails.

The stories of the readings that follow will exemplify how the feelings of shame, fear, and lack of power, manifest into illness. They will tell how hidden shadow agendas rule our actions and how we continually create scapegoats. These stories are all taken from actual readings.

Vickie

The Victim Dance

Vickie is a personal friend of mine. She is a thirty-nine year old woman with a master's degree. She is extremely connected to her spirit, highly intelligent and sensitive. Vickie was brought up in the South and exhibits personality traits of a southern bell. Her personality is well mannered and full of sugar. Vickie's parents play out a passive-aggressive energy dynamic, with her mother acting out the aggressive role. Her mother has fastidiously worked at criticizing and insulting Vickie throughout her life. While Vickie's parents offer constant financial and emotional support to Vickie's siblings, she gets just the opposite treatment from them.

Vickie carries a plethora of victim energy. She repeats the destructive pattern of giving her energy away to others and then saying and feeling, "Look what they did to me." Recently, Vickie purchased a ceiling fan. When she returned home with the fan she called some local electricians to obtain a price for the installation. She had allotted fifty dollars from her budget to have the fan installed. One of the electricians quoted her fifty dollars per hour for electrical work. When she tried to get a specific quote on the amount of money it would take for the installation, the contractor would not commit, commenting that each job is unique with its own set of difficulties. Vickie had fans installed before and estimated that it would only take between twenty and thirty minutes. She stated her thoughts to the electrical contractor and then she scheduled the job.

When the electrician arrived to do the installation, he had not been informed by his boss that Vickie was expecting to pay fifty dollars or that her budget did not allow for more. The man came to her apartment, looked at the work that needed to be done, and then he left her apartment to return to his car to get his tools. He did not return until twenty minutes later. Upon his return, he began a conversation with Vickie. She tried to ignore the man. She knew that his clock was ticking and she was trying not to encourage a conversation so that he would get to work. She continued to focus on the work that she was doing all the while that he was talking to her. At least twenty minutes ran by. Finally he began the installation, which took him another half hour. When the job was complete he asked for seventy-five dollars. Vickie looked at him and declared that the installation had not taken him more than an hour. She told him that she should not have to pay more than fifty dollars for the hour that the boss had quoted her.

The man got angry and called his boss, who told Vickie that he had been very clear that she would be charged fifty dollars per hour for the man's time for however long it took him to complete the job. Vickie wrote the seventy-five dollar check, told both of them that it was highway robbery, and said goodbye to the electrician.

From the moment that Vickie wrote the check she began to steam. When she told me the story, three days later, she was still steaming and sure that she was taken advantage of. When I asked her if she knew that she had the responsibility to pay him while he was chatting with her, she said, "Yes," and explained that she was trying to ignore him to hint to him to get to work. When I asked her why she did not simply tell him that she did not want to pay fifty dollars an hour to make conversation, she gave me a blank look. Her eyes were telling me that this kind of blunt truthful confrontation was something that she was very uncomfortable with. After all, this was not the way a polite southern bell should handle herself. How could she be rude to this man?

When I asked Vickie if she wanted to pay twenty-five dollars to be friendly, she told me that she thought it was the electricians professional responsibility to be efficient. "Apparently not," I said. "If you did not feel that you owed him the money, then why did you write the check for seventy-five dollars?" I went on to explain to Vickie that the way that I saw it (not from a victim perspective) she had three choices. Firstly, when the man first arrived she could have politely stated that she hoped that the job could be done for the fifty dollars that she allotted in her budget. Secondly, she could have pointed out to him that she preferred that he get right to work because she had limited funds. Thirdly, she could have insisted that he spend no longer than an hour doing the installation and therefore she would only be responsible for giving him a check for the fifty dollars that she felt he deserved. These were choices that were apparent to me, but not to Vickie. Instead of taking control, speaking her truth and acting on her convictions, Vickie chose to buckle under and give her power away along with her money. She allowed the man to make seventy-five dollars for a fifty dollar job. I saw her as the victim of her own silence. She had the power to control the situation and make it an efficient job or to choose to allow the man to spend more time than necessary and feel powerless.

The problem was that Vickie was trained by her tribe to be polite. She was trained never to confront. Her aggressive mother had created a passive daughter. In fact, Vickie's passive programming was so strong that even though she knew what was happening, Vickie felt helpless to change her behavior patterns and speak up when it was necessary. Vickie was taught to always put the other person's feelings and desires before her own. The thought of having to change her behavior was so painful for Vickie that she could only allow herself to see that the electrician had taken advantage of her. It was so much easier for Vickie to be a victim than to take charge, speak up, and God forbid, put her self interest before his.

These victim lessons will repeat again and again until Vickie learns to recognize that she is the power behind her reality. She must take a direct look at the tribal belief that truth and confrontation are enemies. She must decide that she counts too, and be willing to take responsibility for her own well-being. She must learn to connect the dots between her behavior and the constant resulting victimization. She must find a way to question the benefits and the disadvantages of relying on her counter productive learned behavior. Finally, Vickie must decide to notice when a situation calls for her to make a decision to change her old behavior patterns.

While these solutions sound simple, they are incredibly difficult to grasp for the individual suffering from leaks in the third, fourth, and fifth chakras. Lack of self-confidence, self-love, and self-respect affect our ability to speak our truth. I suggested to Vickie that she work with her inner child in meditation to create the missing confidence and self respect from her childhood. In a parallel reality, Vickie has the ability to encourage her inner child to speak up while she listens and validates the inner child's verbal expression. In this way, both the adult and inner child can role-play some much-needed behavioral change.

Harry

A Hidden Agenda

When Harry came to me for his first reading, he had just moved to town from a large metropolis located about an hour to the north. He was out of money, lonely, and feeling down on his luck. He confided that part of the reason for his visit was because he doubted whether or not he was in the right business. Having held a high corporate position for most of his life, Harry had recently begun a new career as a business and life coach.

In the course of our conversation prior to the reading, Harry told me that he had scheduled a blind date after the reading to have lunch with a massage therapist that I knew of. This practitioner had a way of convincing people that she was a miracle healer with a unique answer to their problems. Her energy drew in those with illness that wanted desperately to have someone else fix them. She would cleverly lead her clients to feel that they had to return to see her regularly for a dose of her magical healing. I had done readings for a number of her clients and had observed that they would praise her special healing abilities as they went back for her services week after week. Their conditions, however, would remain the same all the while she was mesmerizing them with words of her own power to fix them. Her energy had the hooks of co-dependence. Her methods were diametrically opposed to the teachings of the guides, which are geared towards self-empowerment through spirit connection.

After Harry told me about his luncheon appointment, I felt a twinge in my stomach. I knew that my reading would give Harry a push toward self empowerment and was a bit concerned that he would not have time to process the reading before exposing himself to a heavy dose of energy from this practitioner. In my observation, this lady's agenda offered a quick fix, false security, and deception. I did not say anything to Harry about his planned luncheon, feeling that it was not my place to interfere in his personal life. By the end of my second reading with Harry, this rendezvous made a lot more sense according to the Law of Attraction.

Harry was an attractive divorced man in his mid fifties who looked to be in his mid sixties. The fact that life had worn him down was evident to me. During his first reading the guides recommended that Harry take a *Course in Miracles* to learn to understand the power of the ego voice and to begin the process of learning to discern the voices within that motivate and control behavior. Books were recommended to educate him about poverty consciousness versus perceptions of abundance. He was told to continue his business coaching because of his extensive business experience. He was also told that he did not have the necessary understanding to be coaching people about how to run their lives because he did not have a clue as to how to create peace, happiness, and well being for himself.

While scheduling his most recent visit, six to eight months after his first appointment, Harry expressed his continuing difficulty with money and said that he could only afford a short session. He said that he was beginning to receive messages from the spirit world directly. He wanted to be sure that his messages were coming from his spirit and not his ego voice. He was very proud of the fact that he had written an article and a poem for the local metaphysical publication. He claimed to be very happy and feeling very good about himself. He told me of all the friends that he had made in the *Course in Miracles* and how his life had taken an incredible turn for the better after he had seen me. I could tell from his energy that he was reveling in all the attention that he was getting from the women taking the course with him and from the church where the course was taught. His interest in New Age philosophies had obviously provided him with a common ground and an abundance of single available women.

During his session, Harry asked if he should file for bankruptcy. He had obviously not made any progress with his poverty consciousness or his financial situation would have improved. When I looked at his energy field I saw that his third chakra had a huge energy leak. Harry understood that his negative bank balance was reflecting the heavy negative energy that was lodged within him. Harry was feeling high because he was reaching out for external validation and getting it from every direction. When Harry was receiving attention and validation from another, his emotions would soar, but when he retreated into himself, they would sink.

Halfway through the reading Harry revealed the real reason that had motivated him to schedule a reading with me. He told me that he had begun to work with a new practitioner whose field was negative energy release. He wanted validation from his guides that he was doing a good job of cleaning up his energy field. He said that he felt compelled to schedule three sessions with this therapist the following week to get the job done. He wanted the guides to confirm that he was on the correct path. I told Harry that life was ongoing as was one's internal healing work, and that there was no reason for him to be in such a hurry. From my own healing work, I am very cognizant of the time required between sessions to process issues. It can be a waste of time and money to schedule these sessions too closely together.

While Harry was speaking, his energy felt twisted and false to me. Harry was wearing a mask that even he believed was real. His ego had craftily blended his desire for a quick easy way to clear the profusion of negative energy with his desire to mate. Harry's quick, easy solution to his energy leaks averted his having to face and resolve his painful issues of lack of self worth. Harry had a hidden agenda. Rather than working to develop himself into a person that was worthy of his own self-respect, he was searching for a mate to validate him and serve his needs. His true motivation for the reading was to get confirmation from his guides that this practitioner was the right romantic partner for him. He wasn't sitting in front of me to grow or even to heal as he had stated. He really came hoping that I would foresee a budding romance. The guides went to work to shine the light of truth.

I asked Harry if he knew why he had scheduled the first negative energy release session and how he had come to learn about this kind of therapy. The first answer that he gave was to tell me that I had recommended this work for him. When the guides told me that I had not done so, he concurred that I had suggested that he do this clearing work on himself, but that he had thought this would be an alternative answer. Again, I asked how he had heard about this kind of therapy. He answered that the practitioner had told him about it, and he thought that he would try it.

As Harry spoke, I could feel the dark energy of deception permeating him. He repeated that he had been through one grueling session the previous week and had scheduled three more for the following week. All the while that Harry was lying to himself and to me, the guides were showing me the truth. Harry very much enjoyed the session that he had already had. I told him what the guides showed me and with that information he gave me a confused look. "How could I have enjoyed it when my issues came up?" Again I asked, "If you did not enjoy it, then why are you going back for more three times next week?" By this time the light was beginning to seep through Harry's self deception and the guides signaled me to tell Harry what I saw in his energy field.

Harry had reveled in a full hour of undivided attention and nurturing that he received from this female practitioner. Not only did he have her undivided attention during the session, but afterward he had gobs of material for conversation with his women friends in the group. Conversations about his healing sessions allowed him to spend lots of time talking about and focusing on himself and his life. Harry's need for mommy was being fulfilled tenfold. His endless need for attention and nurturing was being completely satisfied. In fact, it felt so good that Harry wanted to do it three times a week.

Finally the guides asked the jackpot question "What does this lady look like?" "Oh, she is very pretty," he said with a twinkle in his eye and a look that said, "she is for me." At that moment my clock went ding. I looked at Harry and I said, "Stop lying to yourself and your guides. You are obviously not interested in healing or feeling whole. Dating and therapy do not mix well. If you want to date this woman, then you should be honest with yourself and her. Why don't you ask her out for dinner instead of going to her office pretending to want to heal so that you can spend three hours with her to gain her attention, understanding, and sympathy? You are not healing your insatiable need for external validation. In fact you are increasing it with this deception."

Harry looked me dead in the eye. He said, "I prayed and prayed this morning for the light to come. I knew that things were getting worse and that something had to change. I asked for the light of truth and now I have received it." Harry gave me an intense look of shame, expressed his struggle with seeing beyond his own self-delusions, wished me well and left.

Harry was entrenched in playing out a charade that would keep his true agenda hidden. By creating the appearance of wanting to heal, Harry had found a golden hook with which to reel in lots of available women to assuage his feelings of loneliness and need for attention and validation. New Age lingo provided his ego with a common language with which to communicate with women. Under the auspices of wanting healing, he was actually just seeking a mate to fill up his emptiness. Learning the lingo and using it to feed a status quo, dysfunctional, negative energy pattern is diametrically opposed to doing the work of reconnecting with your inner Spirit-Self. There just isn't any substitute for truth. Harry had learned the language well. He was skilled with talk, but he did everything in his power to avoid the walk.

Harry chose to use his limited funds for three sessions of false satisfaction with his intended sweetie. He made an unwise choice to invest his money and energy in feelings of lack. He chose to seek a relationship based on false pretenses because he was hiding from his true fear of failure and inadequacy that kept on manifesting repeatedly as his reality. Then when reality would reflect his negative feelings about himself, he would seek someone to heal him.

The problem that Harry faces is that he will continue on a merry-go-round of continuous seeking, never to find lasting results, because every relationship he begins will eventually reflect the unhealed sense of lack that he holds inside. Until, that inside hole is plugged and Harry learns self-validation, love, and acceptance, true lasting external validation and love will continue to elude him. The movie *Groundhog Day* is a very good example of this lesson. I have discussed this scenario in the section on the fourth chakra.

Karla

More Victim Lessons and Hidden Agendas

I recently did a reading for young mother named Karla, who was in the midst of an outbreak of herpes. She asked me, "Why did this disease sit dormant for ten years as if it wasn't there and then suddenly become such a problem for me?" I told her that her energy revealed that she needed a catalyst that would bring her suppressed feelings of shame to the surface. At the time of the outbreak she was feeling shame that her business had failed, which resulted in causing her to declare bankruptcy. She also felt shame and fear that her marriage was failing. When she was given this information she confided in me that while she still loved her husband, she feared that she no longer liked him.

As the reading progressed, it became clear that the outbreak of herpes had a purpose that aligned with Karla's will. The outbreak gave her the power to push her husband away when she no longer felt close enough to him to be sexually intimate. She agreed with my observation and said, "Yes that is true, although I did not want to admit that to myself." At that point in the reading she could see that she was not an innocent random victim of this illness, but that her energy had played a significant part in activating this disease to serve her hidden needs.

Karla went on to ask me what I saw for the future of her marriage. Karla's husband was a product of a family with negative and limited thinking. His energy field reflected that he was in a negative energy spiral. He emitted very heavy victim energy. She confided in me that for years he complained that everything in his life always seemed to fall apart and that he felt powerless to stop it from doing so. Her husband did not understand how he was actually creating his own living hell. His negative approach to life was to try to find a job that served his needs and then find reasons to complain about it, rather than to choose to create a life that included work that he enjoyed. He was a habitual complainer.

I explained to Karla that when I looked toward the future, I saw windows of opportunity. I saw that she had an opportunity to use the information that I had given her in the reading about how one creates a personal reality based on positive or negative energy. She had a new opportunity to teach her husband about the negative and limiting energy that he was creating, and about the power he had to create change and share with her a more satisfying, positive, joyous life. I also saw the opportunity for her to admit her true feelings to herself and to her husband with the intention of creating a more honest and intimate relationship.

Each time there is a window of opportunity to change the momentum of the present blueprint of energy, there are new alternative possibility lines that follow. This is what I saw for Karla. I went on to explain to her that if her husband did not choose to respond to the new opportunity that she presented to him to grow and change, but if she did, and she continued to desire to be a part of a positive relationship, that she would eventually attract a man to her that would have a harmonious compatible energy to hers.

At that time, however, her husband's fearful, limiting, passive, powerless feelings were perfectly mirroring hers. The Law of Attraction, like attracts like, was working well. The victim feelings that she was processing in her first chakra were feeding the outbreak of herpes. However, if Karla chose instead to release the limiting, passive, powerless feelings, then she would open a window of opportunity for herself to move forward toward her own health and happiness.

When a person is facing a window of opportunity for change that is crucial to the development of a relationship, often, I cannot see where the energy is going beyond the point of the window because the formative, free will choices have not yet been made. This was the case in Karla's reading. She would have to take the responsibility of making the decision about her marriage based on how the relationship unfolded when she applied the results of her new found knowledge and positive changes in her own perspectives, thoughts, and behavior.

As for the herpes, Karla's body was trying to notify her of her own feelings of shame, fear, and stress connected with the denial of having the power to take charge of her life and make it into what she wanted it to be. In the reading, we dealt with new career choices. We addressed the fears that she was building that she would not be able to support herself if her marriage failed. She began to think about taking a step in the direction of creating a new career goal.

The key to Karla's recovery was in her ability to address her own feelings and fears, and to deal with them in a proactive way. At the conclusion of the reading Karla thanked me and said that when she called me, she had been feeling desperate and powerless. She said that now she was feeling very excited about the future and felt that the reading had already made a positive change in the way that she viewed her life.

When I spoke to Karla six months later, she was preparing to take a long vacation in the South with her family. She said that even though her husband had not changed his behavior since her first reading, her perspectives had changed. She had decided to return to school, but did not want to make definite plans until she relocated to a place closer to her extended family. She was living in the Northeast and had realized that she was unhappy living so far away from her mother. Karla's need for nurturing and support, which was ignored by her husband and in the past had contributed to her depression, was now drawing her towards those in her family that gave the needed support with ease. Karla's family would be able to provide additional nurturing and support for Karla's son, which would give Karla more time and mobility to pursue her new career goals. Karla was making plans to relocate and was in the process of gathering information to help her husband to find a new job so that he would be willing to make the move.

Instead of feeling trapped, frightened, and whining about her problems, Karla had taken charge of her life by deciding to look deeper into her feelings and come up with alternative positive solutions for change. She called me the second time because her son was having trouble in the private school that he was in and she wanted to know if she should home school him. She was concerned that this would drain her time and abort her new career goals. She said that she did not know of any other school that seemed right for him in her present vicinity. The guides suggested that she hire a temporary tutor for him. They said that she should not invest too much energy in home schooling, but instead that she begin to look for a school in the town where she planned to relocate.

It was clear that on a spirit level Karla's young son was providing her with more ammunition to relocate. This was her heart's desire. She needed all the help that she could get from the universe to convince her stagnant husband to pull up his roots and make the change. The child's well being would certainty be a motivating factor in her husband's decision.

In Karla's case, the universe was doing its job. By creating an educational dilemma for her son in her present location, the guiding force was giving her the incentive to follow through with her desired relocation plans. Even though I knew that the external energy was actually reading Karla's script, I told her that it appeared that the universe was giving her the guidance and support that she and her family needed to point them in the direction of a healthier and happier life. When I pointed this out to Karla, we both chuckled like two little girls that share a secret. At times like these I can feel the fullness of the "All That Is" pushing the joyous energy through my heart chakra. I knew that Karla felt it too.

Linda

Creating a Scapegoat

Linda called me way in advance to schedule a reading on Valentines day. The day before her appointment, she called to express concern that she did not have enough money for a full reading, but she said that she felt conflicted because she knew that she needed one. We decided to do a short reading where we could focus on her business, the one particular area of concern to her.

The reading revealed that Linda was concerned about the state of her new herbal business. She and her husband were about to invest a substantial amount of money into the business that was hanging on by a thread. She wanted assurances that she was doing the right thing by increasing their financial investment. She asked if the business would succeed. When I explained to her that she would create the success or failure of the business with her energy, she complained to me that her husbands attitude was so negative that it pulled both of them down. She felt that it was his negative energy that was causing the downfall of the business. Her energy field revealed both the cause of her dilemma and the solution to it.

Linda was a middle-aged woman who had married her second husband a few years prior to the reading. Her husband had a successful medical practice and was appeasing her by spending much of his free time helping her in her new business. Linda had insisted that her husband work in the business with her in his spare time. Silently, he resented having to give up personal control of his free time and consequently hoped the business would fail. He lent her outward support and money, but his feelings of resentment were building.

I suggested to Linda that she release her husband from the business, and go it alone. She replied that her husband would leave her if she were not available to share his leisure time, especially in the evening. She declared that she only had two choices if the marriage was to last. One was to give up the business. The other choice was to include him in it. To the contrary, the guides suggested that she had plenty of time to run the business when he was at work and that she did not have to work in the evenings.

It become clear from her energy that Linda was manifesting her issues of inadequacy and abandonment. She was extremely co-dependent and was terrified at the suggestion of handling the business by herself. She admitted that she did not feel that she had the ability to function in the business without her husband because she relied on his abilities. Her husband had become her scapegoat. Blaming him was simply easier than dealing with her issues.

The guides were showing me that as long as all the energetic variables remained the same, the business was doomed to fail. While Linda had the passion and belief for the amazing healing effects of herbal remedies, her husband had absolutely no belief or conviction in the remedies and did not belong in that business. He had invested his belief in pharmaceutical medications. I suggested that since the business was born of her previous personal success with herbs that she jump into the business on her own and learn to swim.

The guides showed me that if Linda took responsibility for her own happiness, relied upon her own passion, was willing to release her fears, by releasing her husband from the business, that the business would thrive. If she did not make these changes, she was throwing good money after bad and doomed to fail. I explained how she was in the process of setting herself up to face her fears by creating circumstances of failure and abandonment. With every attempt to circumvent her fears, she was actually affirming their power over her and bringing them closer to manifestation.

Again she asked me, "But doesn't the business have a chance?" "The business will be what you make it," I replied. With that the time was up and I ended the reading feeling that she had not allowed herself to absorb even one ray of light. I mailed her an audiotape of the reading and said a prayer for her. I hoped that perhaps if she listened to the words four or five times that maybe some understanding of the concepts of energetic creation would begin to seep in.

The fact that the reading was scheduled on Valentine's Day lead me to believe that this reading was a lesson in how we use our partners as scapegoats who hold excuses for our own reluctance to make the difficult choice to release the fear that is connected to our perception of lack of ability. When we choose, instead, to release the scapegoat and gather the courage to deal with our issues, we are catapulted towards feelings of empowerment and reconnection with the full potential of our Spirit-Self.

Susan

Smoke and Mirrors

The first time that Susan called me, she was conflicted about whether or not to continue her relationship with her boyfriend. The guides informed me that the energy dynamic of the relationship arose out of blocks on her energy field that were located in her lower right career center, the area between the first and second chakra. The blocks were lodged in the area that processes the energy of safety, security, money, and relationships. In addition, the energy in Susan's entire left side, all the way to her left foot, appeared to be blocked, indicating that she was completely cut off from her sense of feminine creative power. She felt powerless and unable to see or initiate any alternate choices in her life.

As it turned out, Susan was 42 years old and thinking of leaving her job. Her job duties consisted of assisting a paraplegic who was totally paralyzed on the left side with slight ability for movement on the right side. Her employer appeared to be a physical reflection of Susan's blocked energy field.

When Susan went to work for her boss, she was in school studying to become a physical therapist. It was there that she met a woman who offered her the job of caretaker. She accepted the offer and quit school.

At the time of her first reading, Susan was involved in a two-year romantic involvement with a married man whom she insisted she loved. He spoke of his twenty-five year marriage as a happy one. He had three children, two of which were young adults and still living at home. He could not face the fact that he had outgrown his marital relationship. Rather than dealing with his marital difficulties, he chose instead to have a relationship with Susan on the side. He had ended the relationship with Susan numerous times with a declaration that he did not want to hurt her by staying with her, but each time he had returned. The night before the reading he declared another ending to the relationship with Susan.

When I looked at my inner screen, I saw him returning. When Susan heard this, she wanted to know if she should take him back when he returned or if she should make the ending final. The guides indicated that there was no point in taking drastic action with the relationship because it was accurately reflecting what was going on inside of Susan. I saw that if she released her boyfriend, she would draw in another unsatisfying relationship to match her energy field script.

Susan was on the correct path to finding her inner strength, self-respect, and independence when she was attending physical therapy school. If she had completed that course, she would have had the ability to leave her boyfriend and the job at any time that she desired. Instead she sabotaged herself and found herself without any educational training or any clear alternatives. She found herself paralyzed to make the necessary changes in life because she could not see any other options. Her unwillingness to use her creative energy was indicated in the huge blocks in the left side of her energy field.

Although Susan claimed that she wanted a healthy committed relationship, she chose an unavailable man who fit perfectly into her energy script. Susan's father was an alcoholic who was never around for her in her childhood. Her energy field held the belief pattern that men disappoint and do not provide safety and security. Consequently she found a man who could not be there for her because he had other obligations. She, like her father, found every way that she could come up with to escape facing her true emotions about her feelings of inadequacy and was reaching out for a relationship to mask those feelings, rather than to address them and follow through with action to develop her abilities and her self respect. Susan had inherited her father's karmic issues.

Throughout this book I have continually said, "all is one." In this case the messages and the guidance that were available for Susan were all around her. The universe was screaming at her, but she was blind and deaf.

Both Susan's boss and her boyfriend were mirroring back to her the choices that she was making in her life. In this case the Law of Attraction, like attracts like, was obvious. Susan's boss was mirroring her stagnant situation. The entire left side of Susan's energy field was blocked, as was her boss's nervous system. In addition, her boss's physical state of paralysis was a perfect reflection of the fact that Susan could not find a way to stand on her own two financial or creative legs. Susan had picked a romantic partner who mirrored her complete denial about taking responsibility for one's happiness and well being. He would not face the fact that he was not happy in his marriage. He refused to confront and deal with his marital situation, his sense of honor, and his life. He felt guilty about his behavior towards both his wife and Susan, and he remained in complete denial about the negative energy that he was creating for himself and his family.

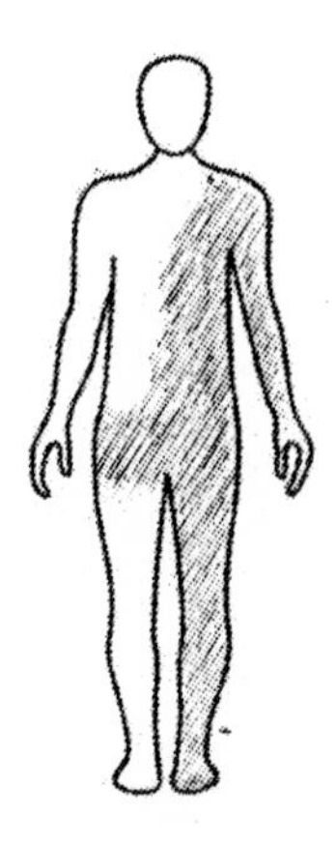

SUSAN'S HEALTH SCAN

The guides suggested that Susan quit her job, go back to school to complete her physical therapy education, or choose some other form of career training. They pointed out that with the ability to find satisfaction in her career that she would be able to build self-respect, and then she would be more apt to make a wise decision about her relationship. When Susan felt better about herself and her abilities, her relationships with men, with this man or another, would begin to reflect her internal fulfillment and satisfaction with herself.

Six month's later Susan called me for another reading. She had not made any changes in her relationship or her job. Her boyfriend had returned shortly after her first reading and the relationship had continued until the day that she called to ask me if she should break it up because he was married and she was beginning to admit to herself that it bothered her that the relationship appeared to have a dead end. She felt that she wanted more time and attention from her boyfriend than he was able to give to her. She finally admitted that although she knew that he was married, she had hoped that he would leave his wife for her.

Again, the guides suggested that she take care of her career, her feelings of self worth, and her self-respect before making any final decisions. They reiterated that in order for her to change the outside reflection, she needed to first change her internal feelings about herself. The guides added that if Susan chose to move forward by facing and dealing with her issues, that the new energy might open a window of opportunity for her boyfriend to do the same.

By focusing on wanting Prince Charming to rescue her from her responsibility to create a happy and fulfilling life, Susan was giving her power away. She needed to learn how to rescue herself. In fact, Susan was using this relationship to distract her from dealing with the issues of personal growth and development that were facing her.

I do not know whether or not Susan has made any changes since I last spoke to her. I do know that there are thousands of Susan's, some of which I speak to every day. Some choose to open their eyes, face their fears, and take action; others do not.

Lisa

Inherited Karma

When we are blind to the negative, limiting, belief patterns that we hold, they have an insidious power to cause feelings of frustration and unhappiness. When we learn to identify repetitious patterns, we gain the ability to harness the power to work within our energy field to make positive changes in our underlying beliefs. With the recognition of the patterns that reflect our energetic scripts, we develop the ability to exit from an uncomfortable ride on our own personal karmic merry-go-round.

Lisa is a thirty-eight year old woman with a husband and two children. Lisa's karmic lessons were screaming at her through the past and present events in her life when she called me for her reading.

By the time Lisa completed her reading, her patterns and the lessons contained in those patterns were crystal clear. Lisa's scan showed:

- A large block in the neck area and throat chakra.

- Blocks in her shoulders, the upper left nurture center, and down her left arm, indicating that she felt a lack of nurturing from her mother and a lack of power in being female, due to not having a positive female mother model.

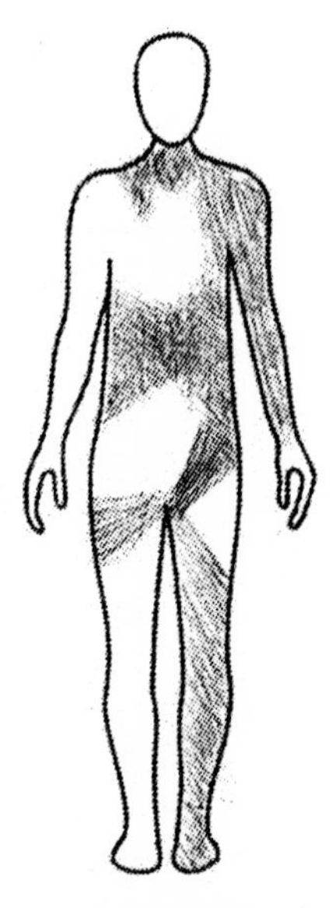

LISA'S HEALTH SCAN

- A block in the third chakra on both her right and left side, indicating a problem with self-love and self worth.
- A second chakra block, indicating that she was storing a secret.
- A first chakra block showing energy leaking towards both the right and left sides of her energy field, indicating family difficulties and inherited victim patterns.
- The left leg was blocked, indicating that she was not using her female energy and did not have any respect for it. She had difficulty in relating to female energetic behavior and power.

- Blocks in her upper right shoulder, indicating a feeling of a lack of nurturing from her father.

- Blocks on the lower left side, indicating a lack of ability to create alternative choices.

- Blocks on the lower right side, indicating a feeling of lack of power, particularly with men, both in her past and her present.

Lisa's energy field also revealed an inner child splinter that emitted a large amount of trauma from a time when her mother almost died. Not having anyone to help her deal with her emotions and fears was very painful for her. This pattern of emotional repression strengthened its development throughout her life.

At first when I told Lisa about the blocks in her nurture center she could not relate to any lack of nurture from her mother. Then the reading revealed that when she was a small child, she and her brother had to be very quiet because her father worked at night and slept during the day. Everyone in the home had to tip toe around on behalf of her father. The pattern of putting the patriarch first began to emerge. "We don't count," was the program that the children in the house learned. The children were stifled from having loud expressive fun. They had to learn to hold back their natural impulses to speak up.

In Lisa's family her mother was the boss. Her father had very little to do with the children. Lisa said that her mother wanted to work and be more active outside of the home, but she never followed through with her desire because she knew that the concept was considered unacceptable to Lisa's father. Lisa said that she saw that this frustrated her mother. By giving her power of choice and responsibility for her happiness over to her husband, Lisa's mother set an example for her children. She taught her children the following beliefs:

- The man is the king of the castle and makes all the important decisions.
- Men must come first.
- A man's health and desires count and a woman's do not.
- Women must make sacrifices for men.

Repetitious Patterns

At the time of the reading Lisa worked for a software company with mostly male workers. She conveyed that she thought it was inappropriate when the women workers would cry and express their feelings in corporate meetings. Lisa said that she preferred to do the job well and not act like a woman.

When Lisa told me of her feelings about her female co-workers, she was illustrating her negative judgment about emotional expression. This attitude was the result of her history of stifling her own emotions in her youth. I suggested to her that maybe these women needed to be heard, and that they might have had something valid to express.

Lisa believed that women do not have any power. This first chakra leak was feeding a case of endometriosis. The illness represented a rejection of Lisa's own female energy. She held the belief that men get what they want, but that woman's desires don't count. This belief was the root cause of her feelings of weakness and unworthiness, and lead to the rejection of her feminine essence.

The second chakra blocks revealed that Lisa was in the habit of aborting the formation of her own ideas, hopes, and dreams. This too was an inherited behavior pattern that she learned from her mother.

The blocks were root beliefs that were attracting some very stressful, unwanted events into her life. The following events, however, did present opportunities for Lisa to change her negative and limiting beliefs about herself, her femininity, and her relationships with men.

Six months into her pregnancy with her second child, Lisa's husband had a motorcycle accident and broke both his wrists. Consequently, Lisa had to take complete care of him. She resented not being able to put her attention on her baby and her pregnancy.

Lisa's husband was mirroring her energetic history. Lisa's husband had inadvertently left his kickstand down when he accelerated his motorcycle. The kickstand was located on the left side of the bike. When he leaned into a left turn, he was thrown from his bike, breaking both his wrists. The kickstand was symbolically representing the block in Lisa's female energy in her lower left quadrant. Her husband was part of the design to cause Lisa to replay the inhibiting behavior and resulting negative emotions from her childhood that were the original causes of her blocks.

Remember that in her childhood Lisa had leaned that she could not express her true feelings. After her husband's accident, Lisa again found herself in a position where she felt that she had to remain silent about her feelings. This time she had to turn her attention away from her own children and focus on their father, the patriarch. At the time of the reading, two years subsequent to the accident, Lisa confessed that she still felt resentment that her husband had drained her energy, and she felt robbed of the time, peace, and serenity that she thought she deserved in her pregnancy. She wanted to know how to release the resentment. That was the secret that she held in her second chakra. Lisa had never told anyone how she felt. She stored this negative energy in the area of her endometriosis.

Inherited Karma

The inherited karmic cycle was repeating in the following ways:

1. During those difficult months, Lisa had to take attention from her daughter and re-assigned most of her time to her husband. There was little that he could do for himself with two broken wrists. The child learned that she was not as valuable as her father. The negative belief pattern was passed from Lisa to her daughter. The child learned that the patriarch is more important than she and that he is more deserving of attention.

2. Lisa remained silent about her emotions, just like her mother had done.

3. Lisa felt powerless to make the choice to put her time and attention where she wanted it to be. Her mother had held on to the same feeling.

At the time of the call, Lisa's eighty-one year old father was suffering from an advanced case of Alzheimer's disease. The family, which consisted of her mother, grown sister, and brother, was again totally wrapped up in focusing on the patriarch, instead of their own nuclear families. Lisa was overcome with guilt. She felt that she was not seeing her father often enough because there was a distance of three thousand miles between them. She spent a lot of time thinking about him and feeling guilty. She carried an air of sadness. She brought those emotions into her household and again took her time and attention away from her children to focus on the patriarch. This time Lisa's father was not taking her power away. Lisa had learned to give it away.

Lessons to Learn

The third chakra processes lessons of self-love, self-respect, and self-worth. Lisa was blocking all of these positive feelings. Instead of positive energy, her third chakra was full of guilt. In order to correct this, Lisa needed to learn discernment. She needed to learn that there are times when it is okay to be selfish and to put personal interests and children before parental problems. When Lisa learns that she counts too, she will stop brushing herself aside for others. When she makes this change, her energy will no longer draw in circumstances where her happiness and well being have to compete with and take a back seat to that of another person.

The reading went on to reveal a war between Lisa's male and female archetypes. The endometriosis on the right side was being caused by her inner male energy rejecting her female energy. Lisa needed to get in touch with her own inner goddess energy. She needed to learn that her female energy has value and that it deserves expression. That discovery would go a long way toward putting her male and female energy back in balance which would be reflected in her external relationships.

Lisa also needed to learn to pull the focus of her energy away from her father when she was not visiting him and to decide not to think about him all the time. She needed to learn to believe that her happiness is just as important as everyone else's. In order to take responsibility for that happiness, she would have to put her focus on the joy in her life, not just the trauma. The joy would multiply the positive energy, whereas the sadness would multiply the negative energy. Simply put, her lesson was to learn to choose peace over feelings of worry and guilt.

Recommendations From the Guides

- It was recommended that Lisa do inner child meditations in which she encourages her inner child to express bottled up emotions. She was told to redo the trauma of her mother's near death, but in the new parallel reality, Lisa was to add lots of loving, supportive, nurturing, female, energy for her inner child. (See Chapter 7, Healing Methods and Therapies.)

- Lisa asked how she could stop from passing the negative karma on to her children. She was told by the guides to validate her daughter's words, thoughts, and ideas. She was told to ask her daughter to express her opinion more often, and to treat her with the respect that any individual, large or small, deserves. She was also told to stop giving the message to her daughter that her father, brother, or grandfather are more important than she is. In addition, she was told to do these same things with her inner child splinters in meditation.

- It was recommended that Lisa take a course in Reiki. When doing hands on healing on her own body she would be validating herself. Reiki is a healing art that activates internal healing energy. The practice of Reiki also helps to open up receptors for meditation.

- General meditation was recommended as another female energetic activity to help clear her second and third chakra blocks.

- A specific meditation whereby Lisa could call up and talk to her male and female archetypal parts was recommended. The female part of her needed to speak and be heard.

- Because of the guilt, grief, and lack of opportunity to express her emotions throughout her life, the guides made a recommendation that Lisa seek some form of talk therapy to help her through this difficult time with her father's illness, and to help her learn how to express her feelings to her husband.

Jane

The Ego Plays Tricks

When I received a call from Jane, she told me that she was suffering from constant, severe confusion that was paralyzing her life. She was very concerned because her kinesiologist was certain that she had a chemical imbalance and was recommending that she begin a program of estrogen and progesterone. Jane had extensive experience with hypnotherapy, herbs, meditation, creative visualization, emotional release work, and other alternative health modalities. She was hoping that I could confirm to her that hormonal therapy would solve her problems. She was forty-five years old and had not yet exhibited any symptoms of menopause.

Before I agreed to do the reading, I notified Jane that I would not be able to give her advice on medications or hormonal therapy because I am not a doctor. I conveyed to her that I was regularly assured by the guides that consciousness controls the chemistry of the body, not the other way around. She was being advised by her kinesiologist to put the cart before the horse. His methodology was to treat the symptoms and ignore the root causes. I informed her that I could shine some light on the issues that were registered in her energy field so that she could address the root causes that were manifesting confusion. She was convinced that she had done all the necessary work to clear her field in the past and had a difficult time believing that her confusion was related to her issues. Surprisingly, she requested a reading anyway. Jane's scan was very complex.

- Blocks were located on the top of her head. I felt sick and dizzy when I scanned this area.

- Blocks were located at the top of her ears. She confirmed that her ears had been burning.

- Blocks were located in her shoulders and her left nurture center, indicating that she felt a lack of nurturing from her mother.

- A block in the left arm indicated a feeling of not having a positive female mother model and a lack of power in being female.

- Blocks were located in the throat chakra, which is the location of the thyroid gland.

- Blocks were located in her upper right shoulder. They indicated some particular form of lack of nurturing from her father. However, her right nurture center was mostly clear of blocks, which indicated that she did receive significant positive nurturing from her father. She later confirmed that her father was her primary nurturer.

- Blocks were located in the right hand, indicating blame towards men.

- Her grandfather appeared in my inner visual screen to be standing in back of her father throughout the reading.

- Blocks were located from the groin to waist on left side. These blocks indicated a lack of feeling safety, security, control, and power, particularly with men, both in her past and her present.

- Blocks in the first chakra held the energy of deep feelings of victimization and shame that revealed childhood sexual abuse.

- Blocks down her right leg indicated difficulty in functioning in the outside world.

- Diagonal blocks were located in the second chakra, creative center. They ran across both the left and the right side, indicating a lack of ability to create a fulfilling life.

- An unusual rectangular shield appeared from the third chakra down to the shins and ran across the entire body. When I probed the shield I felt a sense of isolation and disconnection to her stored emotional energy.

During the scan, when I felt the energy of the inner child, I developed a nauseous feeling emerging from a recipe of repressed emotions including anger, fear, despair, loneliness, and isolation. I discovered that Jane held feelings of self-loathing and self-annihilation. She yearned for an escape from life's difficulties. I also learned that as a child, the abusive, disturbing arguing of Jane's parents had traumatized her. This explained the restrictions in the energy flow that I observed around her ears. Her inner child had created them to block out the disturbing noise.

As I stayed with her inner child, I felt as though I could not breath. Jane confided in me that her energy field had accurately recorded her early childhood trauma of sexual abuse by her father. She was unaware of whether her grandfather had participated, but she was sure that her father had inherited this behavior pattern from him. This explained why her grandfather had been appearing to me to be standing directly in back of her father throughout her reading. He indicated a clear case of inherited karma. When I entered the energy of her fifth chakra, I felt like I was being smothered. The sexual abuse had occurred when Jane's father took her into the shower at the age three and forced her to have oral sex. This event was clearly at the root of her problems. It explained the feelings of dizziness, confusion, and lack of breath that I felt. It also explained why I had the feeling of being on the brink of passing out, as well as my initial sense of being around water.

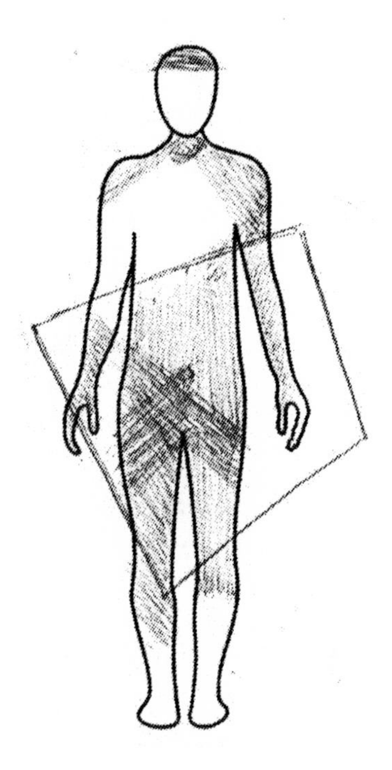

JANE'S HEALTH SCAN

The blocks in her fifth chakra were due to numerous causes. As a child, Jane wanted to speak up and tell someone in her family about her trauma. She wanted to ask for help. The blocks were also due to the feeling of having her throat blocked and her breathing restricted. She confided to me that she had tried to tell her mother about the incident, but that her mother did not want to listen. This accounted for her feeling a lack of nurturing from her mother.

I must admit that both Jane and I were concerned with the fact that she had done extensive work to clear the negative energy connected with this early traumatic sexual violation from her energy field, including forgiving her father and expressing her feelings to her family in her adult years. She told me that until the last decade, she had no memory of her early traumas. She could not understand why all the work that she had done to clear the negative energy had not cleared it permanently, and why it would be bothering her at that particular time.

Jane had previously done a past life regression where she saw that she had been a victimizer in another lifetime. This knowledge caused her to feel that the early victimization in her present lifetime was an effort by her soul to balance her past behavior. Jane thought that by taking responsibility as both the victimizer and the victim, she had done the work necessary to release her from the judgment and pain held by her soul. I could see that it was not helping her, but hurting her. Instead of releasing the pain, she was creating more guilt by feeling that she had invited the abuse for the purpose of soul balance.

Clearly, the symptoms that were interfering with her life were coming from the feelings generated from the early trauma in her present life. Two questions remained. What set off this new episode of confusion? Why was this old trauma still showing up on her field after all the work she had done to clear it?

As I went deeper and deeper into her field, I found extensive guilt regarding a younger sister, brother, and mother. She knew for a fact that her younger sister had suffered the same painful sexual violations. While she admitted that she did not know if her brother was a victim of sexual abuse, she did suspect that he had been abused too. The energy revealed, and Jane confirmed, that her brother was experiencing an intense disruption in his life regarding both his family and career at the time that Jane called me for a reading. I had found the answer to the first question. Her brother's difficulty was the trigger that set off the new episode of debilitating confusion resulting in Jane's call to me. When the harmony in her brother's life began to break down, Jane took the responsibility onto her shoulders and created a new batch of guilty feelings related to the old events.

While Jane had forgiven her parents, she, as well as her inner child had not yet forgiven herself for the acts of omission from her past. She felt responsible for her brother's adult problems because she felt that if she had exposed the truth in her early years, she might have averted her father's subsequent attempts to abuse her siblings. She felt that had she spoken out, the course of the lives of all of the people in her family would have been greatly improved.

Impressions of her younger brother kept appearing throughout the reading. Jane's energy revealed that her inner child held the belief that she was the cause of the problems in her parent's marriage and their constant arguing in her childhood. She felt that her existence was detrimental to all of the members of her family. When problems arose in her brother's life, she did what she had learned to do so well, to take responsibility and create guilt. Even though Jane had done extensive healing work to release blame and embrace forgiveness, She had not released the guilt that calls for self-forgiveness. The shield was a symbol of the block that she built to separate her from feeling the pain of stored emotions.

The act of taking on guilt for the experiences of five other people is a masochistic act of self-punishment. Victim consciousness attracts victim circumstances. Each soul is responsible for its own energy, which manifests into personal reality. We cannot know all the facts that brought the other souls in her family to the circumstances that they experienced. More importantly, we do not have the power to rescue other's from their past experiences. We do, however, have the power to manage, create, and control our own energy in the present moment.

The reading revealed that both Jane and her inner child needed to release the accumulated feelings of guilt. Jane needed to give the other members of her family back their baggage (responsibility for their own lives.) If, indeed, she chose to believe that her mistakes had caused negative repercussions in the lives of others, it was time to confront the feelings and forgive herself so that she could abort the habit pattern of self-punishment and let go of the pain. Clearly, Jane had learned many lessons from her past. She had learned the value of speaking up. She needed to recognize that she had suffered enough. She had very little energy to function well in her adult life because all her energy was being eaten up by guilt and shame. There was hardly any energy left to live a satisfying life. That brings me to the second half of the solution.

Clearing up the negativity in the energy field will release the power that one has to manifest desires in the now moments and in the future. However, to blueprint for a fulfilling future, the individual must generate positive creative thoughts and desires regarding the future. Many people cannot get out of the past because they empower their negative history to keep them focused there.

For Jane, creating guilt and manifesting punishment in the form of physical symptoms were familiar. So was the process of healing. In the past, her healing work had become some of the most meaningful, satisfying, and enlightening work of her present lifetime. One must be careful that this deep satisfaction does not lead to the creation of a healing addict. This sense of fulfillment turned out to be a large part of Jane's problem. Healing can be a very challenging and fulfilling activity. When given the choice of cleaning up the past, or creating new positive life experiences, many people unconsciously opt to stay with what they already know, rather than face the blank canvas of their lives and take responsibility for creating future happiness.

The reading went on to reveal that Jane had not worked for five years because she said that she felt too sick to work. Though she spoke of enjoying her work, the energy revealed that it did not excite her or give her the kind of pleasure that her self-healing work did. When I confronted Jane with feelings of boredom in her chosen work, she confessed. When I asked her what she wanted for her life and herself in her future, she said, "Enlightenment." "But what about life?" I asked, stating that enlightenment is a product of living ones life.

The guides suggested that Jane take on new challenges, like a hobby or some classes to introduce her to some new areas of interest. A new career or a new goal can lead to miraculous cures because they motivate one to begin to harness energy into new positive visualizations. It was suggested that along with the self-healing and inner child forgiveness work that was recommended in the reading, she explore what it would take for her to create a balanced life full of things that she would enjoy. In this way she would be pulling her power to create away from her wounded inner child splinters and would allow the adult to take control. By taking charge of her adult life she would begin to take responsibility for her health and happiness in the present moment.

Jane's illness was not just calling for her to heal old wounds, it was pulling her focus back to the negative past as a clever avoidance tactic for dealing with the present and future moments of her life. I find this to be prevalent in elderly people. Boredom, passivity, the need for attention, and illness all go together like the ingredients of a peanut butter and jelly sandwich.

Let me sum up by addressing the second question directly. Why was all of this old trauma still showing up on her field after all the work she had done to clear it? The answer is twofold. Firstly, Jane still had a dysfunctional inner child. Even though she had done some inner child work in therapy, Jane had not actually accessed the real inner child splinter. In order for that kind of work to be affective, it must be done either in a deep meditation or a hypnotherapy session. Talking about the inner child is not a substitute for accessing the real splinter and working directly with it. Part of Jane's problem was that she manifested illness because it was the only way that her inner child knew of to receive some much-needed attention and nurturing. The huge block in her fifth chakra, often found with childhood sexual trauma, indicates grief at the loss of innocence. More work needed to be done with Jane's inner child until she was able to grow and integrate with the adult Jane.

When the inner child splinters off, it not only doesn't want to grow up, it doesn't know how to grow up. Taking responsibility for creating a happy, well - balanced life is an adult task that requires both work and skill. Jane's adult self had not yet acquired these skills. I have seen many creative varieties of distractive, avoidance tactics due to the fear of failure, lack of healthy adult models, and not knowing where and how to begin to take responsibility and action for one's happiness.

If I had stopped the reading after exposing all the negative energy in Jane's field, I would have walked into Jane's trap to distract her from dealing with her adult fears. I would have validated her dysfunction and given her plenty of satisfying, powerful, healing work to do on her inner child. This would have given her a false sense of purpose. It is true that her inner child would have successfully attracted the much-needed attention and nurturing, but what about the adult Jane? She was in the midst of great suffering also? All the medicine and therapy in the world would not cure her symptoms if they were accomplishing a self-defeating hidden agenda.

The purpose of the confusion that was overtaking Jane's mind was to mask her fear and lack of knowledge about how to go about creating a satisfying life. It would be incomplete to say that the lessons of Jane's life were about victimization and forgiveness. Jane's lessons also included learning how to activate her power to create happiness. When she could muster up the courage to focus on exploring her innate talents, abilities, and potentials that would lead to self-development, then she would be able to use her power to create health and happiness.

Part III

How To Change Your Internal Program

Chapter 7

Healing Methods And Therapies

There is nobody in your energy field but you. Personal empowerment involves clearing and cleaning the smoke and mirrors so that you can see what you are projecting and attracting to you. In order to stop doing the victim dance, we must learn that life is an exercise in consciousness. The truth is that you are only a victim of your own mind. If you want to improve your quality of life, then you need to become conscious of who you are, how you think and feel, and what motivates your behavior. You must be vigilant concerning your negative thoughts, feelings, beliefs, and judgments, at every moment of every day. You will also want to begin clearing old negative energies and learn how to function without creating new ones. The goal is to become an active conscious creator of your desired reality. This requires work.

Summary:

How Health and Happiness are Created and Destroyed

1. Your body is an electromagnetic field of vibrating energy.

2. Energy has a positive, negative, or neutral charge.

3. Positive energy creates health and happiness.

4. Negative energy blocks the creation of health and happiness. Negative energy comes from feelings emitted from the ego voice that are stated on the "I Am NOT" list. Fear and worry are negative energy.

5. The physical reality is constructed out of energy vibrating at a slower rate.

6. Energy works according to the following principles:

   1. The Law of Attraction: Like attracts like. This means that positive energy attracts positive people, events, emotions, thoughts, feelings, and whatever is needed to maintain health. Negative energy attracts the negative people, events, emotions, thoughts, feelings, and illness.

   2. The Law of Abundance states: That which is multiplies.

   3. Law of Balance states: Energy seeks balance. Dynamic energy seeks equilibrium.

7. When negative energy clouds build in your field they block the positive flow of energy required to create health.

8. If negative energy is in your energy field, either you accepted it or you created it, in this life or another, whether or not you are aware of it.

9. Nobody but you can clean up the negative energy in your field permanently. Cleaning requires processing your emotions and taking responsibility for your energetic charge. This requires the release of negative beliefs, judgment, blame, guilt, and fear.

10. If you don't know that negative energy is being stored on your magnetic energy field, then is has the power to work insidiously to make you ill.

11. Illness is the way the body signals you that there are blocks in your field. Think of it as e-mail and be grateful for the knowledge. Once signaled, you have the power to make the changes necessary to clear them, if you choose to do so.

Readiness is an essential ingredient to healing. True healing can only occur when the old patterns of creating and empowering negative energy are outgrown and there is a readiness to release them. Here are some clues to your readiness. Are you:

1. willing to invite change?

2. willing to take responsibility for life?

3. willing to release identity as the victim?

4. willing to release the past and recognize the power to create reality is in the present moment?

5. willing to let everyone else off the hook?

6. willing to change your judgmental perspectives, attitudes, opinions?

7. willing to release attachments to wounds and self pity?

8. willing to release fear and embrace peace?

Healing Is A Two-Step Program

Part One: Clean and Release

In order to heal, we must first own our issues, problems, feelings, perspectives, beliefs, and fears. The path to healing involves acknowledging, feeling, and processing emotions. We must release negative energy and replace it with positive energy. The following list contains suggested methods for activating the healing process.

1. Dialogue With Yourself

The ego is a professional defendant. Remember that the ego hides and the ego lies. Sometimes it is necessary to act like a lawyer and cross-examine the hostile witness, your own ego. Ask yourself the difficult questions.

- What is really going on here?
- What am I feeling?
- Why am I feeling this way?
- What emotions am I hiding?
- Who am I blaming?
- Who am I judging?
- What is my true motivation?

- What expectations did I bring to this experience?
- Is this a repeating pattern?
- Why did I create this event? How does it serve me?
- Is my ego (fear) controlling me?
- What shadow issues are other people mirroring back to me?
- Is this what I truly want or what others want for me?

2. Listen To and Journal Your Feelings

Often we don't know our feelings. How can we own them when we don't even know that they are there? Talking to a friend can allow you to hear your own voice and learn when hidden anger and resentment are present.

3. Rituals for Release of Negative Energy

1. Negative energy can be released through intention combined with action. Verbally affirm your intention and then try this ritual. Write down all negative judgments and emotions that you are feeling and burn the paper that they are written on. Have an intention that as they burn you are willing to allow them to disappear forever.

2. When negative energy release work is done, it is necessary to create positive energy to fill up the resulting

empty spaces. How about replacing the negative energy with energies of compassion, love, understanding, and acceptance? What other energy would you like to include? Verbally affirm your intention. Give these energies a color and a form. Visualize your body absorbing these new positive energies, and then make your own list of energies that you wish to embrace as replacement energy. Remember, the energy that you carry and emit into the universe will reflect back to you.

3. Write a letter to the person or persons that you are angry with. Express all your truthful emotions so that you may know what they are. Read the letter and then determine if you feel that you need to express your hurt feelings to the other person. Perhaps you can read the letter out loud and listen to yourself. Sometimes it helps to read it to a friend and discuss it.

When you have processed your emotions you will be in a better position to determine if you need to express your feeling directly to the person, mail the letter, or dispose of it. When you are finished, you can opt to burn the letter or throw it out with the intention of releasing your judgments and negative emotions, for your own sake. After you have processed your emotions you may determine to make a change in your behavior. Perhaps you will choose to speak your truth or change another behavior pattern. When one person changes the energy dynamic in a relationship, the other person will usually do the same.

4. Create your own rituals for forgiveness and the release of fear and judgment.

4. Rebirthing

Rebirthing is a process of peeling away the layers of the ego's illusion of separateness. It is a therapy that helps one to accelerate soul growth through transitional times. Deep breathing is used as the method of clearing and reconnecting to the spirit.

Release of resistance to change is processed through the fifth chakra. When the release is complete, the free flow of positive energy through the fifth, sixth, and seventh chakras allows the clear digestion of new concepts and ideas for a more authentic life. At that time, changes are welcomed and the person feels uplifted and eager to proceed forward with life.

5. Prayer - Dialogue With God and the Universe

State your intention to call your spirit out of judgment. Ask for help. Your support group of friends, family, angels, and guides in the spirit world are very careful not to interfere with your free will. When we pray and ask for help, we are offering them an invitation to spring into action to help us to direct the energy so that we may achieve our goals. Asking for help is not the same thing as saying, “do it for me.” The universe will light up alternative choices, send information, and infuse positive energy. However, the supporting entities will not interfere with your free will choices. Making changes and taking action is still up to you.

6. Create a Positive Energy Field

1. Create positive affirmations that begin with the words "I am." Some examples are: I am light, I am love, I am happiness, I am health and I am prosperity. Louise Hay's book *You Can Heal Your Life* is chock full of positive affirmations that really work to transform your field.

2. **Crash Therapy** - When in the midst of a negative energy spiral, take cover by getting out of your own way. A powerful force of destruction is created by the proliferation of negative thoughts and perspectives. The way to turn the manifestation around is to see and affirm abundance, though the external world may clearly appear to be exhibiting scarcity. The only way to turn the energy vortex inside out is to pull your power out of your belief in the apparent reality of your situation. Affirm that you own the power to create and have a God given right to do so. Then use your power to affirm and visualize what you want, rather than what you see. It takes practice, lots of motivation and courage to look poverty in the face and proclaim that you have the power to manifest and are participating in an abundant universe. You must discipline yourself to not believe your eyes by digging way down deep and attempting to get in touch with your God-Self, power point. Then you must pay attention to the ideas that bubble up that indicate some form of positive action must be taken.

At the crucial beginning stage it is necessary to be on constant vigil that what you see, think, and say is positive. You must eliminate all your judgments of yourself, other individuals, society, and God. Creating positive energy in the midst of a storm is hard work. With a little time and practice it can become fun, and so can your life.

When you have managed to move beyond the crisis, it would be a good idea to search out the original energetic root causes that paved the road for the crises. Crises are wake-up calls to process unfinished business. Just because a crisis has passed does not mean that you should resume life as usual. There is still more clean up work to do in order to break negative creative habits.

7. Project Awareness Into the Pain

Remember, all energy is intelligent. The point of this exercise is to get the body to tell you what it has been trying to get you to notice. Close your eyes. Take some deep breaths and focus on the location of the symptom or pain that is occurring. Project your consciousness inside of that area. Tell your body that you know that it is trying to deliver a message to you.

Tell it that you are ready and willing to listen to its message. Then stay relaxed and wait. Pay attention to any concepts, emotions, and memories that come into your mind. Also pay attention to any other form of message that might come to you right after you open your eyes and begin to return to your regular activities. The form could be anything from telephone solicitation to a sign on a truck.

8. Meditate

Meditation is a tool that takes many forms. To be effective, a good meditation must refocus your attention from your external reality to your internal reality. While many of my clients tell me that they meditate, rarely do they tell me that they are able to see and hear from their guides in a meditation. The following procedure will lead you to a place that is called the Living Waters. The Living Waters are healing waters. This is a place where it is possible to learn to communicate with spirit guides and friends on the other side, as well as to do deep healing and release work.

MEDITATION PROCEDURE:

1. Light a white candle.

2. Create positive affirmations. Some examples are: I am peace. I am love. I am health.

3. Ask the universe for guidance and protection. Ask that only the highest and best come through.

4. Send love and light out into the universe.

5. Sit upright with palms up. You may wish to hold a clear quartz crystal in your hand to amplify the reception.

6. Take three deep breaths and rise up...up...up. Use your breath to give you a feeling of being pushed up by a jet pack. See yourself picking up speed until you feel like you are traveling up at the speed of a rocket.

Go up until you see a waterfall. If your left brain is fighting you and you do not see a waterfall, then you can jump-start your right brain by imagining one.

7. See yourself entering the healing waters. Meditate either from the body of water or directly under the waterfall.

8. Look for your guides. If the entity that you are with does not feel like a guide or an angel, then you might want to go to a higher level. In that case go up some more. Dismiss anything that does not feel like it is there for your highest and best good. Watch and listen to your guide. Always ask for more clarity if you need it. If you feel like you are loosing the focus, do more deep breathing. Resist the ego's attempt to create doubt by convincing you that you are imagining what you see. Instead, decide to trust what you see. Eventually, with practice, you will learn to discern the difference between what you are receiving from a higher level and what your personality is creating.

9. To close the meditation, thank your guides and close your psychic doors. This is done by imagining a set of double doors closing at the very top of your head. You might choose to say out loud three times, "I close the psychic doors."

10. Drink clear water after a meditation.

11. Additional instructions include:

- Meditations should usually not last longer than one hour.
- Never meditate under the influence of drugs or alcohol.
- I suggest that you play the *Inner Journey* Hemi-Sync tape sold by the Monroe Institute while you meditate. (www.monroeinstitute.org)
- For people who find that they fall asleep during meditation, I recommend meditating in the bathtub.
- You can go to the Living Waters just prior to going to sleep to release stress and negative energy.

9. Creative Visualization

The following healing methods are creative visualization techniques that must be done in a deep meditation or hypnotherapy regression to be effective. Be creative. Creativity activates energy that is stuck. Visualization is a way to inject new positive energy and push out the old stale energy of negative memories and experiences.

While in a deep meditative state or hypnotic state, the subconscious mind cannot determine the difference between real and imagined, therefore the imagination can be used as a tool to experience the much-needed emotional fulfillment and empowerment. We have the ability to use our imagination to create new positive habit patterns that replace old negative patterns. If you create a new internal pattern, you will begin to exhibit the pattern externally as well. Athletes use this technique when they practice their athletic form in their minds.

1. Return the Baggage

Visualize returning dark negative thoughts and beliefs to your parents by seeing yourself giving them back their dark luggage. This is the equivalent of saying, "I refuse to take on your negative and limiting beliefs." Send love, compassion, and understanding, but refuse to carry their negative patterns containing perspectives of lack.

2. The Negative Energy Drain

This exercise is particularly helpful when you are in a negative energy spiral as discussed in Crash Therapies. A quick drain of negative energy can be done prior to the conscious creation of positive affirmations.

This is a way to clean up your psychic space. To drain your house and body of negative energy in a meditation, imagine that you and all living people, animals and plants are levitated up to the ceiling. Then drain all of the dark energy out of an imaginary drain in the center of the room. When all of the dark energy is gone, fill the room with white light from above and allow the living forms to gently float back down to their original position. Follow with lots of verbal positive affirmations.

3. Forgiveness Therapy

Visualize yourself in a room alone with each person that you feel that you need to forgive. Tell each individual whatever it is that is causing you to feel angry. Look the person directly in the eye. Seek to understand why they treated you in a way that was unacceptable to you. Open up your heart to receiving understanding that is stored for you on spirit levels. Tell that person that while you do not sanction the particular behavior, you are going to release your negative thoughts and judgments connected with him/her. Proclaim that in doing so you release them and set them free and that you also release yourself and set yourself free. You might want to follow up with a visualization of cord cutting.

4. Cut The Cords

Cords are real phenomena on a spiritual level of being. A dark cord keeps people tied together in a relationship that reflects shared negative energy. Decide to break free from the agreement in lack. Cutting a cord is a short cut to learning the true energy dynamic of the relationship. An honest intent to cut a cord requires a sincere desire to feel whole and complete and release feelings of need, denial, and judgment.

During meditation ask your guides to show you what dark cords exist between you and the person causing you difficulty. Thank the person for participating in your lesson and release him/her from the soul agreement. Then cut the cords close to your body and close to the other person's body. Throw the cord into the Living Waters and ask the angels to remove the roots.

After cutting a cord, one must pay attention to gentle thoughts of truth about the relationship that may come to mind throughout the subsequent twenty-four hour period. For example, if you have become a scapegoat for another, or vice versa, you will become consciously aware of the details of the energy dynamic. If the intentions are not honest and the person fails to come into a new and deeper perspective, the cord will be reset by the same person or a different person. When the lesson isn't learned, it will be repeated, in this lifetime or another.

5. The Bridge of Light

This is an exercise intended to create inner peace and forgiveness. Visualize yourself standing on one side of a bridge of light with your Higher Self (a personification of your highest Spirit-Energy minus the ego-energy) standing next to you. See the other person that you have an issue with standing on the other side with his/her Higher Self. Meet in the center of the bridge. Talk to the other and express your feelings. Allow the other person to answer you. If you cannot find peace in your meeting, then turn to either Higher Self and ask for some insight. Stay with it until you can find a way to release the other person from the debt that you are holding on to. You do not need the other person's cooperation to find peace within yourself. Be determined to release all of the negative energy that you hold regarding the other person before you leave the bridge. Send love and light to the other and go on your way.

6. The Round Table - Parts Therapy

This can be a very enlightening and healing visualization. Convene a meeting of personifications of your archetypes and personal parts. Try to identify and get to know each one. Some examples might be your ego, heart, inner children, male, female, inner parents, artist, queen, tyrant, past life personalities such as the aristocrat, pauper, nun, priest, and prostitute. Give them each a chance to express their feelings, fears, and desires to you. Accept all of your parts, including the shadow personalities that you are inclined to reject and banish. Tell them that you are perfectly happy to listen to their desires and consider their feelings, however none of them may have total control over the whole of you. Devise a communication system so that you may come to know which parts of you are in conflict and can pay attention when one of them is calling out to you. Thank them all for participating in your human experience. Make a conscious decision concerning which ones you can draw more power from so that you may become more balanced.

7. Inner Child Visualizations In Mediation

Children and Abuse

Sexual, verbal, and physical abuse can occur at any age, but so much of what I see traces back to childhood trauma. When small children are faced with an act that violates their boundaries, they react by feeling small, powerless, and terrified. Much of the terror registers in the fifth chakra area because they feel too afraid to speak their truth. Grief, created from the loss of innocence, creates a block that can appear, and remain for an extended period of time, in the fourth and fifth chakra areas. Clouds from child abuse can begin to register anywhere on the energy field. Hurt, disappointment, guilt, anger, and blame can register in all of the chakras.

The wounded inner child is a vacuum that pulls you into your past. Thoughts, feelings, and memories emerge from the inner child and repeat over and over again. The inner child splinter draws the adult back in time so that the adult part of the personality can recapture the spirit of the child that it left behind. When the inner child is acknowledged and helped, it can begin to grow and integrate into the adult. When the inner child splinters are fully integrated, the adult self will find it easier to live in the now moment where it can utilize one hundred percent of its power to create a healthy and happy life without restriction.

Blocks in the energy field that begin in childhood and reinforce themselves from a lifetime of memories and confusion, remain until both the inner child and the adult parts of the personality can find a way to see the events in a positive light. Our children inherit our own karmic behavioral lessons by mirroring our own inner children. When we heal our own inner child splinters, we are helping to mitigate the inherited karma.

Creating parallel realities is an effective way of working with inner child splinters. A negative energy vortex can be infused with positive energy by creating a positive parallel event. This kind of therapy serves to give the childhood splinters back their feelings of power by undermining the roots of victim energy. This healing method also serves as a way to practice being creative. It is important to understand that a person can benefit from experiencing deep positive emotions, regardless of whether or not the event is real or imagined.

Methods of Healing the Inner Child in Meditation:

1. **Introduce yourself to the inner child as its future self.**
   Ease the child's fears by giving it some assurance that it will grow up and be fine.

2. **Encourage the inner child splinter to use its voice to express.**
   Give the child a safe and secure atmosphere to allow it to feel and process its emotions. Make a regular practice out of asking the inner child how it feels.

3. **Empower the inner child.**
   Redo traumatic events in a new visualization, only this time give the child the power to resolve the situation according to it's desires. For example, if a child was molested, ask it what it would like to do to emerge from the situation in a victorious way. Encourage the child to set and defend its boundaries. Give the child the power to create a solution and then play it out in your mind exactly that way. Always give the child a voice and a sense of power and choice.

4. **Teach the inner child how to use its creative energy.**
   Ask the inner child to decide what it wants to create. The child can draw, paint, create puppets or even change its own body, hair, and clothing. The imagination is limitless, as is the energy with which we create reality. Always help the child to see its many options. The inner children are only children and need to be taught how to think up alternatives.

5. **Give the inner child nurturing.**
   Have the child create loving, nurturing parents, family, and friends. Play out the details of how the parents nurture, validate, support, and express affection. Introduce the child to various kinds of quality time with their parents and with you, the future-self.

6. **Keep in touch with all of your inner children splinters**.
   All children fear abandonment more than anything else. Check in with your inner child on a regular basis. Each inner child splinter will begin

to age and grow as it heals. Eventually when all the dysfunctional splinters are healed, the adult can have one healthy joyful inner child archetype as a part of its personality.

10. Additional Assisted Therapies that can help the individual to release negative emotions and judgments.

1. Neuromuscular and deep tissue massage can help to open pockets of stored memories and emotions.

2. Various emotional release therapies exist, such as SomatoEmotional Release therapy. These therapies can help to release stagnant emotions and replace them with positive alternatives.

3. Hypnotherapy is effective for forgiveness work, inner child work, and parts therapy.

Part Two: Creation

Creation gets the juices flowing in your creative center. Use your right brain by activating the imagination. Ask yourself what you would like your life to contain. Stop relying on others to provide your life for you. Give up the need to smother yourself in the company of others. Use the precious moments of your life to grow and develop who you are. Some suggestions are:

1. Get some physical exercise.

2. Develop a hobby or two.

3. Seek new challenges. Learn new things. Take a course. Stretch your mind and your abilities both physically and mentally.

4. Do something creative: Cook, paint, sew, knit or work with flowers.

5. Explore new places.

6. Rent comedy videos and lighten up.

7. Make some new and different friends.

8. Use your imagination to make your life fun and interesting.

9. See the movie *Ground Hog Day.*

Chapter 8

Evolution

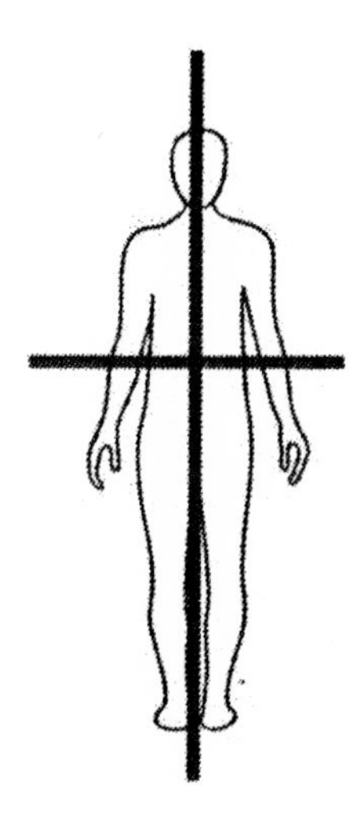

In this book I have talked about the Law of Attraction and the Law of Multiplication. I have explained how energy will attract and project the magnetically charged thoughts and beliefs that we carry. I have stressed the importance of knowing how and what we are creating so that we may play a more conscious part in intentional creation, rather than falling victim to our unconscious creations. However, there is more to the human energy dynamic than just carrying a positive energy, because as I have said, this human experience is about duality.

Throughout this book I have talked about the concept of duality and how the Law of Balance moves energy from one extreme towards its dualistic opposite, much like the swing of a pendulum. I have mentioned the Tree of Good and

Evil, our desire to have dualistic experiences, as the purpose for the existence of both positive and negative energy.

The High Road and The Low Road

HIGH ROAD ____________ **LOW ROAD**

Earlier in this book, I stated that life is a spirit game. In this game there are times that each of us must hold some negative energy. When you are on the high road, you can see the spirit game from outside of the box. From this perspective of higher consciousness you can see that you have a choice which energy you want to create and hold on to. You know that someone has to play the bad guy in every script and that it is not necessary to judge the other person for wanting the role. You can see that judgment is negative energy and choose to pass on owning it. From the higher perspective, it is easy to have compassion for all the souls who are suffering the consequences of their negative energy.

On the other hand, when you are on the low road, you are a player in the game. This requires a limited perspective from inside the box. This is a victim perspective. This is a vulnerable place to be. It is where you are constantly being pitched negative thoughts, beliefs, fears, and perspectives. This is a very turbulent location. If this is your choice, be ready for the drama.

Unfortunately most souls are not conscious of the fact that there are two roads to choose from. I have summarized the beliefs and feelings encountered on each of these paths in the "I Am" and the "I Am Not" lists. If I have accomplished anything in this book, I hope to have helped you to see that you have been making many choices that heretofore you have been unaware of. It is time to WAKE UP and pay attention to your choices.

Why do bad things happen to good people?

POSITIVE ENERGY ____________ **NEGATIVE ENERGY**

THE LAW OF BALANCE

Why do bad things happen to good people? Bad things happen because this is the land of duality. In addition to the fact that negative karmic energy seeks positive energy for completion, the opposite dynamic is also at work. When we have an excess of positive energy, the negative energy tugs at us to create holistic balance. I had a friend in college who used to say to me that every time it looked like everything was going well in his life, God would come along and hit him over the head with a hammer. That is the law of balance in action. The only thing that we can count on in this system is constant change. On the earth plane there will be loss with every change of form. There will be beginnings and endings. People and things will come and go, but if we stay tuned to the "I Am" list, we can focus on the unity, the peace, and the universal support that is there for us. We do not have to see change as loss. We can choose to see it as transformation, experience, and growth. This positive perspective will allow us to maintain and benefit from a positive energetic charge. If we can surrender to the movement of change, then life can be an exciting adventure. Every difficult situation has a silver lining. If you will allow yourself to look for it, then you will discover the reason why we all continue to stay in the game.

What does the game board look like? Well, we know that it is chock full of duality. It must have dark and light areas, because that is the nature of duality. I like to think of it as a checkered game board. The "I Am Not" list is the negative energy of the dark squares and the light squares are the positive energy of the "I Am" list. We also know that there is an underlying male-female concept at play in the human energy field that extends to our bodies, behaviors, and attitudes.

But, there is one more dualistic dimension on planet earth that we have not given our attention to. This book would not be complete without acknowledging the field of time that is part of the game. Time gives us a past and a future, with a gift of experience, the present, in the middle. The subject of time brings forth the following two questions that I hear almost every day. Where am I coming from and where am I going? It is time now to address these questions in a larger sense.

Each of us is living a small story that is part of a bigger story. As individuals we are microcosms. As a human race we are a macrocosm. The macrocosm is called history. If we look closely at history we see that it has a distinctly male quality.

MICROCOSM ———— **MACROCOSM**

As I look at history, this is what I have observed:

- History is named after the male gender = his story.
- History was recorded by men, from male perspectives.
- Human beings are referred to as mankind.
- Ninety-five percent of our historical legends and heroes (our models) are men.
- God is called he.
- Men wrote the bible using the male perspective.
- Our religious masters are men.
- Organized religions are patriarchal institutions that dictate dogma to a large percentage of the human race.
- The patriarchy has repeatedly persecuted individual female spirituality.
- History has assigned power to the male voice and the male perspective.

    1. The world has had a predominance of male political leaders.

    2. The USA, which is the world leader of the 21-century, has a predominantly male law making body and executive branch of government.

- Real means external and physical in form.
- Men have assigned tasks that they do not like to do, such a cooking, cleaning, nurturing, and care taking to women.
- Men have eagerly accepted financial responsibility and power.
- Men empower other men.
- Men have been the protectors of the family and countries.

- Men have created weapons of war and destruction.
- The medical community is a patriarchal institution.
- The male approach to war is to conquer and destroy the enemy.
- The patriarchal medical community sees illness as the enemy.
- The patriarchal approach to health has been to conquer and destroy symptoms (the enemy).
- The male solution for security has actually created the greatest threat to security — nuclear weapons and nuclear waste.
- Men reject emotional expression.
- The patriarchal society has exhibited ingenuity, courage, and great achievement.
- History has been silent and passive about the epidemic of incest, sexual abuse, and prejudicial violence towards women.
- Mankind has ignored the need to nurture the earth.

My conclusion is that history has been an examination and expression of the right side of the personal energy field of the microcosm as well as the macrocosm.

Women (not all, but most) in the patriarchal world have given their power away by:

- remaining subordinate.
- worshipping male leaders.
- acknowledging male power.
- agreeing to be caretakers of children and home exclusively.
- rejecting financial responsibility.
- rejecting all forms of power including, financial, and political power.
- accepting low wages.
- providing free domestic labor.
- not having a voice.
- accepting patriarchal belief systems.
- accepting predominantly male health care practitioners and corporations.
- remaining silent and passive about epidemic pattern of incest and sexual abuse.
- refusing to take charge of their own lives and bodies.
- refusing to use their voice for themselves and other women.

- empowering men and not empowering other women.

The majority of neither men nor women have:

- respected intuition.
- respected meditation (passive reception) as a spiritual practice.
- nurtured and cared for the earth.
- recognized and valued our emotions.

These are all aspects of the left side of the human energy field. If we look back at the diagram of the four quadrants, we see that as a planet we have assigned power to all the male aspects of being human and diminished the female aspects of our being. Simply put, we have rejected our female energy and thrown it in the shadows down in the basement. We are out of balance.

A New Dawn

The following are the changes that I see taking place right now; some are only beginning, others are more pronounced. There is:

- a new emerging respect for the intuition.
- a new emerging respect for the practice of personal meditation and personal spiritual connection.
- a new respect for holistic and natural approaches to health.
- a new respect for nurturing mother earth.
- a growing distaste for war.
- some, but far too little, discussion in the media about incest, sexual abuse, domestic physical abuse predominantly of women and children, and worldwide violence against women.
- a new respect for the feminine voice.
- a recognition that planet earth requires our attention and care.

These are all the beginning signs of an energy shift in mass consciousness. The human race is starting to mature. It is starting to open up to its female creative side. It is beginning to own its true internal, creative potential. But this is not being done directly to the macrocosm. No, what is inside is reflected outside. This change is taking place one person at a time! One by one, we are evolving. As we mature our individual souls, the over soul also matures.

Does this mean that men have something to fear? Are we headed toward a matriarchy? I think not. This is not a revolution; it is an evolution. It seems to me that we are heading towards a state of balance. We cannot get to where we are going without the intention of the males on our planet. Both sexes contain a left female side. Both sexes contain a creative right brain. The time has come for us to be more of who and what we are. It is time to use all of our abilities, rather than fifty percent. Both males and females, equally, have this task set before them as the third millennium dawns.

How do we get there? We can't change the world by making sweeping changes to the countries or the planet. We make changes in the macrocosm by making individual internal changes in the microcosm. Individually, we must retrieve our female side from the basement shadows, clean her up, and learn to love her. Let us rediscover the parts of ourselves that we have denied, ignored, and banished. By changing our individual lives, we create the energy dynamic that will be reflected in the new paradigm of balance. For the first time in recorded history, we will know what it means to feel whole and complete.

What will this new paradigm require of us?

- First and foremost we must decide to be honest with ourselves.
- We must take a new look at the positive aspects of using our female energy.
- We need to get in touch with our internal spiritual connection for guidance. Meditation is a passive form of receiving from spirit.
- We need to look at the pejorative attitudes towards women and decide to change them.
- We need to stop worshiping the intellect in place of our emotions. We need to allow ourselves to respect, feel, and express our emotions.
- We need to take responsibility for ourselves! Both sexes must be willing to hold on to one hundred percent of their own energy and give up co-dependency.
- We must learn to recognize the ego voice that encourages a dynamic imbalance.

Women

Women need to give up the role of slave. Lincoln freed the slaves, but nobody has notified the women of this country that they are free. Women must begin to take their power back and act free! Women must give up the fear of responsibility and of power. They must decide to become examples of courage and balance for the next generation. They must demand that their partners share in the workload. Women need to acknowledge that both fathers and mothers need to parent. They both need to nurture and care for their children, each other, their homes, and themselves. Both sexes need to know how to cook, clean, and care for themselves. Women must STOP thinking that it is their duty to serve men, while nobody serves them. Women must begin to require an equal exchange of energy. With that will come equal pay and respect. Women need to realize that both males and females are entitled to develop their talents and skills. Women need to stop enabling everyone else and start enabling themselves. They must begin to see that both genders must find a way to feel financially capable and secure. Both sexes need to feel comfortable knowing and following their own heart in their own line of work. Neither sex is to become subordinate to the other. Partnership is the name of the game for the third millennium. Women must let go of the deep depression and strong addictive mood medications that they have been given by the patriarchal medical community that keeps them numb to their own thoughts and emotions. We cannot find our strengths and process our emotions until we can feel them. Instead of medication, women need to embrace change. They need to get in touch with and express their feelings. It is time to take charge of your own body. It is time for women to harness their courage and their will to be happy! They need goals, nurturing, self respect, and rest more than they do medication.

Men

Men need to give up the fear of change. Men need to take charge of their egos (fears of losing power). They need to redefine terms like "macho" and "real man," as men that are comfortable with their own feminine side. They need to understand the term "whole and complete." Men need to want to examine and replace the old destructive patriarchal belief systems. They need to stop expecting and demanding that women wait on them. I have noticed a tendency in progressive men to speak the new holistic language, while acting the same old ways. I have seen these traits exhibited in the business world, health care field, and personal lives. It is hard to teach an old dog new tricks. Each individual must be alert to the ego's deceitful methods. Remember, it is the ego's job to manufacture fear. Men must make an effort to communicate by listening to and expressing their emotions. They must begin to acknowledge their hidden fear, anger, and resentment. They must begin to acknowledge and get to know their inner children and other archetypes. Lastly, they must make an effort to give nurturing. Men, too, must harness their courage. They must be willing to learn new nurturing skills, even if they know that their fathers would have laughed at them. Their wives and children will love and appreciate them more for it.

Men and Women

In order for balance to come about, we must all find and face our own shadow. We must seek and own our "NOTs," judgments, and fears. This is what it means to become conscious. Everyone must get to know his/her own mind and heart. We must confront our shame and acknowledge that it is time to come out of the closet. The gay movement has been holding the shadow of denial and self-rejection of female energy for all of humanity. The gay people have been our scapegoats for our lack of love and respect for feminine energy for too long. Women that are in touch with their creative power have been falsely accused of being witches for too long. Instead of acknowledging and respecting our individual feminine energy, we have been projecting our fear and hatred of it onto both groups. It is time to stop. We must make an effort to see and admit our fears and judgments about our own internal aspects. We must learn to respect all of ourselves. Only by doing this can we open up to the possibility of true self-acceptance, love, and compassion.

We cannot change until we decide to let go of the old dysfunctional models. Just because your parents exhibited co-dependent and judgmental behavior does not mean that you have to follow in the dysfunctional path. It is time to open up to a new, healthier way of life. It is time to own our own energy, not half of it, but all of it. When we own all of our energy, we will no longer need to drain it from others. When we own all of our energy, we will not have to worry about having enough money to pay for medical bills in our old age, because we will be healthy. We will not have to worry about money, because we will all be capable of manifesting all that we need and want with the flow of available of positive energy.

Let us not be afraid of the change. The big hand is moving. We all must release the fear. Let us embrace the creative flow of positive energy and enjoy the ride. During these transitional times it behooves us to move forward with a positive attitude and to be open to new perspectives. Our children and grandchildren will be the benefactors of our courageous effort.

To Thine Own Self Be True

Hamlet, Shakespeare

You are the master of your own soul. Reality is what you see and believe to be true, based on what you choose to see and believe to be true. If you are getting a life that is not to your liking, then there is a need to examine the energy that you hold and emit. An honest search for the root energetic causes of the apparent reality will produce truthful results. Identifying thoughts, beliefs, motivations, and payoffs are necessary factors in piecing together the sometimes complicated, conflicting agendas that you carry. You must be sensitive and persistent in your effort.

Above all, the intention to get to know oneself takes effort, courage, and honesty. One must decide in advance not to retreat at the first sign that Pandora's box is beginning to crack. The demons in the box can only unleash as much power as you choose to assign to them. The more that you choose to fear them and hide from them, the more power that you give to them to disturb you.

If you were to hold your hand in front of a light bulb, large shadow figures would appear on the wall in front of you. Yet, the actual size of your hand is relatively small compared to the huge shadow images. In the same way, the events of childhood build their power over time and become relatively large images in the minds of their fragmented inner child owners. Just like the shadow view of your hand, your inner monsters tend to shrink way down in size when you coax them out of storage and look directly at them from a mature adult perspective. Our inner children, the parts of us that still feel like little fearful, abandoned people, hold on to these images even when we attain adulthood. However, we have the power to rescue our own inner children. We can turn the lights on in their isolated rooms so that they can begin learn what it feels like to have inner peace. We, as adults, can provide the nourishment and the space that they need to grow.

The basic lesson that I have learned from all the readings that I have done is that we are all made of the same essence. When we look at the thoughts of embarrassment and shame that push us to hide from our own selves, we can't help wonder what is going on here? We all feel so fragile, and yet we are really so powerful. We appear separate, but we are really one indivisible self, playing a game whereby we make believe that we are separate.

When we judge, criticize, and reject another, we are only pushing away the complex human aspects of ourselves. Human life becomes a much simpler journey when we remember that it is a spirit game and that while some of us will choose to do outrageous things to each other, it only happens when energy patterns match and join together in earth plane play.

We are the masters of our own soul experiences. Some of us will choose to come and go from the earth plane in various shocking, gruesome, and heart wrenching creative ways, at some seemingly inconvenient and hurtful times. It is all an illusion. It is all the gift of experience that we choose to give to each other. The characters in the play may come and go, but the actors and actresses are all the same. Good guys, bad guys, sick people, rich people, poor people, evil people, we have played many parts. What do we fear? We fear loss, without which there can be no earth plane game. We fear being judged. Who do we judge? We continue to judge ourselves, until we reach the one special lifetime where we can see the truth of the unity. Then we stop crying and start to laugh. We laugh when we notice that all the signs, symbols, and clues were always there, right in front of us, all the while that we were searching. We laugh ourselves silly all the way to heaven, heaven on earth.

Learning to remove the judgment and fear from life and replace it with joy is a process. Little by little we can choose to learn to develop the skills that we need to release our quiet, helpless, hopeless feelings of suffering and replace them with joy and laughter.

The journey back home takes intent and effort, but it does not have to feel like work. It can be an enlightening, playful, enriching life, just as Dorothy displayed in the *Wizard of Oz.* The journey will teach you to use your brain (think for yourself), have courage (confront and challenge your fears), and to find your own heart (discover your passion). Your abilities will grow with practice. Rest assured that the power is within you. It always has been, and it always will be. It is who you are. It awaits your discovery.

Life is a journey of getting to know your-self.

Suggestions For Your Journey:

1. Seek to discover who you are and decide to take responsibility for creating who you want to become.

2. Release guilt and judgment and replace them with compassion.

3. Develop the courage to face your fears.

4. Worry and fear are negative energy; be willing to release them.

5. Hold your own energy. Fill your own need.

6. Take responsibility for personal joy and health.

7. Stay in touch with your inner children splinters.

8. Pay attention to signs and symbols that mirror messages back to you.

9. Recognize and release the need for external validation.

10. Dialogue with yourself. Ask the difficult questions. Confront yourself about your true motivations and payoffs.

11. Know that you are not a victim.

12. Acknowledge the interconnectedness of everything.

13. Lighten up. Engage in laughter.

14. Know your power to create and constantly affirm it out loud.

15. Learn to recognize boredom and to use the precious moments of your life consciously.

16. Learn to recognize your fearful ego voice.

17. Live in the now-moment.

18. Be positive.

19. Learn to love and accept all of yourself, which includes the reflective behavior of everyone else.

20. Be kind to yourself and others.

Acknowledgements

I must acknowledge the many masterminds on the other side who have engineered and coordinated this huge task. Thank you to all of the guides and angels that I have worked with who have brought a continuous stream of clients to me. I extend my sincere gratitude to all my friends and relatives who have passed on that have joined with me to add their energy to this effort. Thank you to my friends Billie, Vickie, Susan, and to our master guide Dr. Quan. Thank you to all the clients over the years who have taken the time to call me to tell me that I had a positive effect on their lives; thank you for your encouragement. Thank you to Sandy, Jennifer, Carolene, Melanie, Ileen, Jacquie and Gina, whose encouragement guided me to stay on my path. You will be forever appreciated. Most of all, I want to say thank you to those that have helped me to midwife this book. Thank you to Desiree for opening the Tea Room and to Karen who has shouldered much of the burden of the gestation period. Thank you Karen for the endless hours of telephone talk that helped me to organize the information and for your personal support and friendship. You are a treasure. Thank you to Lindsay for your friendship and for all the encouragement that you have given to me through the editorial drudgery. Thank you to Marilyn, Melissa, and Noelle for doing the proof reading. Thank you to my son Spencer, for never once complaining about all the time that I spent looking at a computer monitor. You are the greatest blessing of my life. Last but not least, thank you to Larry for having been one of my best teachers.

Printed in the United States
53106LVS00002B/90